PAPUA NEW GUINEA

Science

Grade 7

Teacher Resource Book

Kenneth Rouse

OXFORD

OXFORD
UNIVERSITY PRESS
AUSTRALIA & NEW ZEALAND

253 Normanby Road, South Melbourne, Victoria 3205, Australia

Oxford University Press is a department of the University of Oxford. It furthers the University's objective of excellence in research, scholarship, and education by publishing worldwide in

Oxford New York

Auckland Cape Town Dar es Salaam Hong Kong Karachi Kuala Lumpur Madrid Melbourne Mexico City Nairobi New Delhi Shanghai Taipei Toronto

With offices in

Argentina Austria Brazil Chile Czech Republic France Greece Guatemala Hungary Italy Japan Poland Portugal Singapore South Korea Switzerland Thailand Turkey Ukraine Vietnam

First published 2008
Reprinted 2008, 2009, 2010, 2014

ISBN 978 0 19 555517 2

Typeset by Pier Vido
Illustrated by Uramina and Nelson Ltd
Printed by in China by Golden Cup Printing Co. Ltd

Contents

Overview

Science

Science helps us to explore, understand and communicate information about the things that we find in the world. The **scientific method** provides students with a reliable way of finding out about the world and solving problems. The knowledge, skills and attitudes developed by science education will help students to prepare for playing a greater part in their **community**, and for further study or entry to the workforce. Science education helps students to make informed and responsible decisions about their way of life, their health, their environment and the kind of society in which they want to live.

Science for Grade 7 Student Book

Key features

The content of the student book is designed to be applicable to the wide range of learning contexts of students in Papua New Guinea. The success of implementing the science curriculum depends on the abilities of the teacher to adapt the curriculum and learning materials to the context of the local community. Consequently, the content is flexible in that students in both rural and urban areas can relate to the information. Both the text and the illustrations reflect diverse contexts such as islands, highlands and mainland coastal environments.

The content of this book supports student learning for the science curriculum area. The book:

- directly supports and supplements the upper primary syllabus by following the sequence of strands and sub-strands, with one chapter or section for each strand and clearly identifiable topics for each sub-strand
- contains direct references to the new upper primary syllabus at the beginning of each chapter, demonstrating the clear relationship between the student book and the syllabus
- provides topics and learning approaches that directly support the achievement of syllabus outcomes. The subject content is based on the topics listed under 'Recommended Knowledge' subheadings in the 'Elaborations' section of the *Science Teachers Guide*
- includes a wide range of student activities at the end of each topic (which can be completed inside and outside the classroom), reference information and a glossary of terms. Most activities in the 'For you to try' sections were derived from ideas under 'Recommended Skills and Suggested Activities' in the 'Elaborations' section of the *Science Teachers Guide*
- uses icons to indicate where book content has major links to other upper primary subjects and to indicate activities or investigations appropriate for assessment
- is written at a reading level that is appropriate for upper primary students and with a format that allows teachers to use it in ways that best suit their objectives and personal teaching style

- draws extensively on examples that are culturally appropriate to upper primary students in Papua New Guinea, giving recognition and credibility to Papua New Guinean knowledge and skills
- uses language that is gender-sensitive and includes positive gender roles
- uses text as the main medium of the activity-based approach and includes a good proportion of pictures and illustrations to support text
- requires only those resources that are normally available to teachers in Papua New Guinea, especially those in rural and remote areas
- includes summary questions at the end of each chapter.

Science for Grade 7 Teacher Resource Book

Key features

The Teacher Resource Book, in conjunction with the student book, will help teachers implement the science syllabus for upper primary students. It provides teachers with the following information:

- relevant information for planning a school-based program
- topics cross-referenced to other curriculum areas to allow for the development of integrated units of work
- a selection of teaching and learning strategies
- ideas for assessment activities
- topic elaborations to show how to develop topics covered in the student book into units of work
- how to extend and develop relevant content and contexts from the student book
- additional information that will assist teachers to develop their own units of work
- additional projects, investigations and activities to further extend students' skills.

How to use it

In order to make the best use of this book you will need to:

- get a sense of the information it contains and how it is organised
- become familiar with the strands and sub-strands, processes and skills, elaborations of learning outcomes, and teaching and learning strategies
- consider how to use the information to develop your own programs and units of work.

Structure

The Teacher Resource Book is structured in the following way.

- Each chapter covers one syllabus strand for science: (Strand 1: Working scientifically, Strand 2: Living things, Strand 3: Science in the home, Strand 4: Earth and beyond).
- At the beginning of each chapter there is an **overview page** which highlights:
    - ➢ the outcomes of the strand and sub-strands
    - ➢ how these outcomes are developed over the three upper primary grade levels
    - ➢ key words and concepts used and developed throughout the chapter
    - ➢ possible assessment tasks that could be carried out to assess students' knowledge and skills
    - ➢ identified content that has major links to other upper primary subjects.

- **Teacher information**—in this section, information is given which is additional to that already in the student book to enable teachers to develop units of work. A sample unit is also included in the appendices to show how a unit of work can be developed over a period of time to achieve specific outcomes.
- **Equipment** needed for the activities and investigations—this section, with cross references to page numbers in the student book, lists what students will need in order to carry out the investigations, activities or projects in the chapter. Further notes on equipment are listed under 'Useful materials' on page 12.
- **Answers and explanations**—this section provides answers to some of the questions or includes suggested answers or an explanation or elaboration of the text of 'For you to try' questions.
- The **appendices** at the end of this book include:
  - a sample unit of work
  - planning and assessment templates.

A **glossary** is also provided.

- **Icons**—there are icons throughout the student book. The following icons indicate strong links to other subject areas. For example, when dealing with the strand **Science in the home**, there are links to the Personal Development strand: Our culture, values and lifestyle; and to the Social Science strand: Culture. The icons look like this:

ML	ML = Making a Living	M	M = Mathematics
PD	PD = Personal Development	L	L = Language
A	A = Arts	SS	SS = Social Science

An **icon** is used to suggest which activities can be used for assessment: **A**

An icon is also used to remind students to write up a scientific report of an investigation using the headings **Aim**, **Apparatus**, **Method**, **Results**, **Conclusion**. This is explained further on page 13. **SR**

Teaching and learning

Outcomes-based education

Outcomes-based education is used in many countries to identify and monitor progress in student learning. A set of outcomes is written to measure the success of teaching a learning unit, topic or course. These outcomes are measurable and can be used to assess if student learning has taken place. An outcomes approach to education means identifying what students should achieve and focusing on ensuring that they do achieve. It means shifting away from an emphasis on what is to be **taught** and how and when, to an emphasis on what is actually **learnt** by each student.

The impact of outcomes-based programs on teacher planning and assessment has been significant. Teachers have had to shift from focusing on teaching a subject to focusing on planning for student learning.

Learning outcomes

The science syllabus makes explicit the knowledge, skills, attitudes and values that students should achieve in Grades 6, 7 and 8 and these are expressed as learning outcomes and indicators. These outcomes describe specifically what students know and are able to do in each strand and grade. The outcomes are broad and can be achieved in any context depending on available resources and expertise. They are student-centred and written in terms that enable them to be demonstrated, assessed and measured.

A student-centred approach focuses on learning as being the active construction of meaning by students, and teaching as the act of guiding and facilitating learning. Examples would include:

- building on students' prior knowledge
- bringing the community and its resources into the school and providing opportunities for students to go out into the community to learn
- providing opportunities for problem-solving, decision-making and taking action
- providing students with opportunities to reflect upon their own learning, knowledge, values, attitudes and skills.

Learning outcomes are also developmental, showing progression from one level to the next. For example:

6.3.5 Identify and explain how simple machines can be used in homes and the community to do work.

↓

7.3.5 Identify and make recommendations on how simple machines can make life easier through community field study.

↓

8.3.5 Conduct investigations on simple machines and use problem-solving skills to establish the efficiency of the machine as a tool to do work.

Developmental outcomes aim to develop students who are able to:

- reflect and explore a variety of strategies to learn effectively
- participate as responsible citizens in the life of local and national communities
- be culturally sensitive across a range of social contexts
- explore education and career opportunities
- develop income-generating opportunities.

Each learning outcome is illustrated with a list of things that students know and can do in order to show that they are achieving an outcome. These are called *indicators*. Indicators are included in a syllabus to help exemplify the range of observable sample behaviours that contribute to the achievement of outcomes linked to the content. They can be used by teachers to monitor student progress within a level and to make judgments about the achievement of an outcome. It is important not to confuse indicators with content.

Learning outcomes and indicators will:

- give teachers the flexibility to develop programs to meet the needs of their students
- help teachers assess and report students' achievements in relation to the learning outcomes
- allow student achievement of the outcomes to be described in consistent ways
- help teachers monitor student learning
- help teachers plan their future teaching programs

- describe what most students will know and be able to do as a result of effective teaching and learning
- help teachers develop student activities for units of work.

In summary, outcomes provide a scope and sequence of student learning. They provide a useful focus for planning units of work and report student achievements. Indicators assist in the assessment and reporting process. Indicators assist in the achievement of learning objectives.

Strategies

The approach to science is student-centred and provides students with opportunities to practise critical and creative thinking, problem-solving and decision-making. It involves the use of skills and processes such as recall, application, analysis, synthesis, prediction and evaluation, all of which contribute to the development and enhancement of critical thinking. This approach also encourages students to reflect on and monitor their thinking as they make informed decisions and take appropriate actions.

While working towards their goals, students develop communication skills to enable them to work with others to discuss issues, needs, values, feelings, opinions and attitudes. These skills include:

- interpersonal skills of listening, speaking, responding, being assertive, questioning and justifying a position
- skills in presenting feelings, ideas, views, decisions and findings in written or graphic forms or through movement or drama
- literacy skills such as reading, writing and speaking in ways that suit the context and audience, using the specialised language of science.

The following three teaching and learning approaches and related teaching and learning strategies use a student-centred approach.

Approach 1: the 5Es

The 5Es approach is based on the idea that students learn best when they participate in activities that give them opportunities to work things out for themselves. There are five phases.

- Engage
- Explore
- Explain
- Elaborate
- Evaluate.

Approach 2: the interactive approach

The interactive approach involves a partnership in which student and teacher discuss and cooperate in selecting the topic in which the students are then active participants. There are five phases.

- Preparation
- Exploration
- Students' questions
- Investigations
- Reflection.

Approach 3: Predict, observe, explain

In this approach, students draw on their own experiences to make predictions. There are three phases.

- Predict
- Observe
- Explain.

More details of these approaches to student-centred learning are to be found in the *Science Teachers Guide* (pages 8–18).

Teaching methods

There are three main teaching strategies that can be applied for the learning of new information.

Theory learning (i.e. explicit teaching)—The teacher imparts knowledge or demonstrates skills. The teacher accordingly instructs students in what to do and how best to do it.

Practical learning—The teacher demonstrates the steps or processes of undertaking specific tasks. Students observe the demonstration, discuss processes and skills used by the teacher and then practise these skills and processes in a familiar setting.

Experiential learning—The teacher plans for learning to take place in the field or place of work. Here students gain new knowledge as they practise skills in real-life situations. This teaching approach stresses the active participation of students in meaningful activities.

Teachers need to use a range of teaching methods to ensure students not only gain the process skills but can also apply them to relevant real-life situations. Teaching methods to develop these process skills include the following.

Brainstorming—These are activities that are planned to stimulate discussion among students by sharing ideas and opinions on how best to investigate or how best to tackle specific activities and so on.

Surveys and questionnaires—These investigative activities generally go hand in hand with brainstorming. Students collect, collate and analyse data so that they can make informed decisions. A questionnaire is a specific written form where people can record written responses to surveys.

Demonstrations—These integrate sources of information to show specific steps in completing tasks. The teacher demonstrates a process and identifies what research and reporting skills (including the source of information) were used to complete the task.

Discussion/seminars—These teaching methods allow students to clarify thoughts and present information in a logical order within a formal format (seminar) or a less formal format (group discussion). Through exposure to these processes, students develop a deeper understanding of issues/problems and can present informed possible solutions.

Problem-solving—This is a specific process that students can apply to investigate a task for which there is no immediate or obvious solution and establish an action plan to come up with a possible solution. The major steps in problem-solving tasks are:

1. identifying the problem
2. selecting or developing a strategy to solve the problem
3. implementing the devised plan
4. monitoring and recording results
5. evaluating the results.

Presentations/reports—There are a variety of ways a teacher can organise presentations and reports. Reports may be part of a problem-solving task where students present their findings; this may be in oral or written form. They may be individual reports based on outcomes of specific investigative work (written or oral). Presentations by outside sources may be organised to present relevant information for students to use so that tasks can be completed, in particular, large tasks such as projects.

Cooperative group work—Many activities in everyday life require that people learn to work in groups. Through carefully monitored group work, students can experience working as a team. Teachers need to:

- organise their classroom layout in such a way that cooperative learning is encouraged
- plan activities that require students to work in pairs and small groups as well as individually

- construct activities where students consult each other, share ideas and learn from each other. The content to be shared should not be predetermined by the teacher.

Project work—This allows the teacher to create real-life situations where students develop their understanding and skills. They also develop communication skills as they need to talk to each other to reach an understanding. As a group, students have to use and apply basic research skills to locate relevant information as well as organised reporting skills to relay project outcomes. When devising projects teachers need to ensure that projects:

- use real-life or concrete examples
- encourage hands-on learning experiences
- are local and community-based
- provide purposeful and meaningful learning experiences
- promote critical thinking and problem-solving
- encourage interaction with a range of individuals and contexts
- encourage active community participation.

Planning

Planning, programming, assessing and reporting involve the consideration of the individual learning needs of all students and the creation of a learning environment that assists students to achieve the outcomes of the syllabus. Students' achievement of the syllabus outcomes is the goal of planning, programming and assessing. The sequence of learning experiences that teachers provide should build on what students already know and should be designed to ensure that they progress through the levels identified in the syllabus.

In an outcomes-based curriculum, lessons should be planned so that outcomes, assessment and classroom practice are all integrated. Assessment should not be tagged on to the end of a section of work but should be planned at the same time as planning the lesson content and should be ongoing.

Teaching programs need to be developed by teachers to structure learning experiences over a period of time. These programs should consist of:

A long-term plan—such as a yearly plan—where teachers identify and *develop* units of work that will be implemented over a long period of time. Teachers decide on the duration of these units of work in their long-term plan.

Short-term plans—These require the teacher to develop the units of work identified in the long-term plan. These units of work generally are planned to take 2–4 weeks.

Lesson plans—These are generally a further breakdown of the short-term plan (the type of lessons that will be undertaken to achieve the objectives of the short-term plan).

Planning guidelines

Teachers need to plan groups of lessons that enable students to achieve the outcomes described in the syllabus. You should fit each set of lessons into a short-term work plan. Use the following table as a checklist when planning lessons. Planning this way helps to align assessment with outcomes and with practicable teaching approaches in the classroom.

When planning, ask these focus questions.

- What do students need to know and what should they be able to do?
- What do they already know and what can they already do?
- How will I facilitate learning?
- How will I assess learning?

Lesson Planning Table

Outcomes	**Things to plan for**
1 Learning outcome or outcomes 2 Content: topic or key concept 3 What will students learn in the particular lessons? 4 Number of lessons that need to be taught	Identify the outcome in the curriculum that you are working from. To what theme do the lessons belong? (e.g. Simple machines in the community) How will students achieve the learning outcome? List the appropriate: • knowledge to acquire • skills to achieve • values and attitudes to adopt. How many lessons do you plan to teach on this particular topic?
Assessing progress	**Things to think through**
1 Evidence of learning 2 The way learning will be assessed	What will you look for in each student's work? Write down the knowledge and skills that are to be assessed (each one should be something a student can do). Examples of methods you may use: • formal (oral or written presentation) • informal (teacher observation) • small task within a larger project • homework • test.
Classroom practice	**Things to consider**
1 Method or activity 2 Time 3 Teaching methods 4 Resources needed	What will you and what will students do and in what sequence? For how long will you explain or demonstrate new concepts? For how long will students do each activity? How exactly will you arrange students? • as a whole group • working in small groups or pairs • working individually. Where will students be? • in the classroom • outside. List any resources you may need for students to complete tasks.

Assessment

Assessment should be an integral part of the teaching and learning process. Most teaching involves assessment, and by planning what to assess and recording the specific assessment information, appropriate assessment data can be collected.

There are a number of purposes for assessment:

- to collect and analyse information about students' learning
- to provide guidance, feedback and information about students' achievements and progress to both students and parents
- to inform program decision-making and classroom organisational techniques.

The most important purpose of assessment is to improve student learning. Assessment stems naturally from the teaching/learning situation. Teachers in their interaction with students constantly assess:

- students' current understandings
- the nature of any misconceptions
- students' current needs.

Assessing and teaching cannot be separated, and assessment should inform teaching. Assessment is about finding out what students know and can do. The teacher constantly needs to ask these questions.

- What do I want to know?
- How will I find out?

This should be an ongoing process as:

- assessing students continuously enables teachers to monitor closely and understand their progress
- ongoing formal continuous assessment helps teachers diagnose problem areas in both learning and teaching, and allows teachers to change their teaching accordingly
- students receive helpful feedback after every assessment.

Process of assessment

1 Provide students with opportunities to demonstrate what they know and can do in terms of identified learning outcomes.
2 Gather and record evidence of students' demonstration of learning outcomes.
3 Make judgments about students' demonstration of learning outcomes.

Assessment methods

The purpose, principles, and processes of assessment are clearly described in the *Science Teachers Guide* on pages 19–29. Assessment strategies selected by the teacher should be appropriate to the situation and to the purpose of the assessment. Teachers have the opportunity to observe and record aspects of students' learning in a range of situations.

Group work—The teacher can determine the extent of student interaction and participation.

Listening—Listening to students respond to questions as well as other input, the teacher can collect many clues about students' current understanding and attitudes.

Interviewing students—Teachers can collect specific information about the way in which students think about certain situations.

Other assessment methods can include:

- observation
- consultation
- analysis of students' work (examination of detailed evidence in student responses)
- self and peer assessment.

Other sources of information for assessment purposes include the following:

- samples of students' work
- oral explanations or demonstrations to others
- questions posed by students
- practical tasks
- investigations and/or projects
- students' oral and written reports
- short quizzes
- pen and paper tests.

Reporting

Reporting is a way of communicating accurate information about students' demonstration of learning outcomes in a timely way. The purpose is to:

- acknowledge and support students' learning progress
- inform parents about the students' learning progress.

Reporting modes include:

- ➢ written reports
- ➢ student–teacher conferences
- ➢ parent interviews
- ➢ final performance or presentation
- ➢ portfolios.

Science without a laboratory

Science is a practical subject and students should do as much practical work as possible. The term **Investigation** has been used to describe practical work or experiments and this reflects the philosophy of students finding out things for themselves.

While doing practical work, students will learn useful manipulative skills which are relevant outside the science lesson and also learn to solve practical problems. Practical work also allows them to experience the process of science rather than learning only from books. More importantly, practical work is enjoyable and an effective way to learn.

Most primary schools do not have laboratories or special science equipment, but this should not discourage teachers from doing practical work with students. At the upper primary level, science can be taught by using resources that are locally available. These resources include those that are available in the natural environment, things which have been thrown away and can be recycled, and things which can be bought in local stores.

The investigations have been written in such a way that they require only those resources that are normally available to teachers in Papua New Guinea, especially those in rural and remote areas.

Teachers should try out the investigations before the students do them so that they understand the skills needed and the kind of problems that students are likely to face when doing them.

Useful materials

A lot of useful materials are thrown away and can be recycled. Teachers should always be looking for things which can be used to teach science. For example, carpenters and electricians usually leave a few nails or short pieces of wire on the ground where they have been working. Make a collection of these materials and keep them safely in a box so that you have them ready when you need them. You will also need to be innovative and creative to come up with solutions to particular problems.

The students should also be encouraged to think in this way and to collect the materials that they will need for their experiments or to put into the box for later use. Talk to the students at the beginning of the year and also remind them regularly so that they can look for and collect useful materials. Collecting materials in this way will increase their involvement and enthusiasm.

Some suggestions for useful materials to collect are given here.

Glass jars
Glass bottles—various sizes
Plastic bottles (easily cut with a knife or pair of scissors)
Plastic containers
Tins and tin lids
Aluminium drink cans (easily cut with a knife or pair of scissors)
Polystyrene and plastic meat trays
Polystyrene and plastic cups
'Tetrapak' containers—rectangular drink containers that come with their own plastic straw
Plastic knives, forks and spoons
Plastic bags
Wooden and plastic cotton reels
Rubber bands
Pieces of string
Small pieces of blackboard chalk
Short pieces of candle
Old newspapers
Cardboard tubes from inside toilet rolls
Plastic bags
Pieces of material or fabric
Paper clips
Nails
Metal washers
Corks from wine bottles
Pieces of wire—tie wire and electrical wire
Old bicycle and truck inner tubes
Short pieces of plastic or rubber water hose
Magnets—from the speaker of an old radio cassette player, an old computer, an old electric motor or from the rubber strip around the door of an old fridge or freezer
Lengths of bamboo tube or plastic waste pipe
Sand
Cement
Rocks
Fossils

Safety in science

Carrying out investigations in science can involve risks. The activities in the student book have been written with safety in mind and the investigations are safe when carried out sensibly, but there is some level of risk in everything we do. Teachers must take reasonable precautions and ensure that students do the same. Teachers have a duty of care to identify possible risks and take action to reduce the risks.

When students go outside to do investigations in the local area, teachers also need to consider the safety issues involved and remind the students of ways to stay safe. Reducing the risks will ensure the safety of all students and others who may be nearby. When teachers try out the investigation before the lesson, they should also be thinking about safety issues.

Rules for working safely in science

Some suggested rules for Grade 7 science are given below. You might like to make a similar list that is suitable for your students. You could make this into a poster to discuss with your students and display on the classroom wall.

Always work quietly and carefully and be careful of others when you move around the room or whenever you are doing an investigation.
Never run when carrying equipment or near people doing an investigation.
Always read and understand the steps in an investigation before you begin.
Always follow the instructions given by the teacher.
Never taste substances unless you know it is safe to do so.
Tell your teacher immediately if you have an accident.

Writing up experiments, investigations or practical reports

Scientists have special ways of answering questions and solving problems. Scientists also have a special way of writing about their experiments which is related to the scientific method and is called a **practical report** or **scientific report**.

A practical or scientific report gives a list of the equipment and other things that were used as well as step-by-step instructions so that other people can understand what the scientists did and can repeat the experiment for themselves if they want to. Because scientists all over the world use this method, they are able to understand and evaluate each other's work, and communicate with each other. Most reports use the following headings or something similar.

- **Aim:** states the problem, question or purpose of the experiment.
- **Apparatus:** the equipment used in the experiment.
- **Method:** instructions used to carry out the experiment. This sometimes includes diagrams.
- **Results:** the observations or measurements that were obtained. Results are sometimes given in tables or graphs. A discussion of the results may be included.
- **Conclusion:** the answer to the aim or problem being investigated.

Students were introduced to this way of writing up an experiment in **Strand 1: Working scientifically** in Grade 6. Students should be encouraged to use this approach when they carry out an investigation. The **icon** is used in the student book to remind students to use this method regularly. Teachers should continue to check the progress that students are making in this skill and give suggestions about the way that they can improve their writing up of investigations. Being able to write a clear step-by-step report that is easy to understand and shows you can organise ideas under different headings is an important skill in science, and in other subjects. It is just like telling a story with a beginning, middle and an end.

STRAND 1 Working scientifically

About this strand

This strand begins by looking at the meaning of science and then introduces students to **scientific processes** and reminds them about the steps in the scientific method, which were introduced in Grade 6. Students are reminded about the work of scientists in different branches of science and this is illustrated with an example of scientists finding out about the past. The example from the Kuk swamp in the Western Highlands of the first known agriculture in Papua New Guinea also gives recognition to the traditional scientific knowledge of people living up to 10 000 years ago. Students are asked to think about being **fair** in sport and this leads to being fair in science and the importance of designing and doing fair experiments. The idea of **cause** and **effect** is introduced so that students realise that things happen for a reason. This leads into the steps we take in doing experiments to try to find answers to the questions that we ask when we try to find out why things happen. In particular we make **observations**, we make an **inference** and we may make a **hypothesis**. The strand concludes by looking at the ways in which science can help us to understand the world and to improve life in the community.

Sub-strand 1

Main ideas

Sub-strand 1: Critically question their understandings of the broader environment and learn to make informed decisions based on scientific methods.

Key words

Cause, **control**, effect, fair, hypothesis, inference, observation, **reliable**, scientific method, **test**.

Key facts

- People are interested in the things they find around them and often want to find out more about why things happen and how they work.
- When we want to find out about something and understand it better, we often carry out tests or investigations.
- Investigations often start with a question or a problem, we choose a method in order to get some results and then we make a **conclusion**. This way of doing things is called the scientific method.

- When we are planning an investigation we must make sure that it is fair in order to find out why things happen and how they work.
- We often have to make and use simple equipment in order to collect information that will help us to carry out investigations.
- When we have collected information we can use it to make and support a conclusion.
- After carrying out an investigation we should decide if it was a fair test.
- Science can be used to improve community life but the choices that we make must be responsible choices that are based on reliable information.

Assessment tasks

Assessment aims to gather information on how well students have achieved the outcomes of the strand. A variety of strategies should be used: written, oral and practical.

- Each assessment item should be based on criteria that have been clearly written down. Students should be told what the criteria are so that they know the basis for judgment of their achievement and demonstration of the outcomes.
- Assessment should also be continuous and collected throughout the learning process by the completion of appropriate activities such as those indicated with the assessment icon in the 'For you to try' sections.

Major links to other subjects

Strand 1: Working scientifically builds upon ideas introduced in Culture and Community at the elementary level and Environmental Studies at the lower primary level. At the upper primary level, **Working scientifically** links to the strand Health of Individuals and Population in Personal Development. Aspects of different subjects can be integrated into activities such as:

- a project to improve life in the community
- collecting and analysing statistical data for specific groups in the community
- designing posters or performing a drama to relay the message of the benefits of using the methods of science.

Links with other subjects are noted with an icon in the student books.

Teacher information

Teachers should further develop the ideas about working scientifically that were introduced in Grade 6. As well as helping to learn about the world, science is a way of doing things, a way of looking at things and a way of thinking about things.

Teachers should remember that working scientifically is something that should be achieved throughout the Science course. While it is important to teach the concepts outlined in this chapter, working scientifically is not something that can be taught as a separate topic but should be integrated into every topic and activity.

Scientific processes and the scientific method

Scientific processes and the scientific method are important topics that are developed to a greater level of understanding. Students may need more explanation of these than is shown in the book and teachers should be prepared to explain more when needed. In order to assess the students' level of understanding, teachers will need to ask questions of the students. Teachers will also be able to assess understanding of these concepts by the way that they design and carry out investigations and the ways that they try to solve practical problems both inside and outside the classroom. Teachers should also remind students that not all the processes or steps are used all the time but we can select from them depending on the situation.

The work of scientists

The table showing various branches of science and the topics that can be included in that branch should give students some understanding of the wider range of different subjects that can be included. Teachers should understand that this table is not the only way of looking at science and different branches may be included or left out depending on the purpose. For example, archaeology is included here because of the methods that were used to find out what happened at the Kuk swamp thousands of years ago. However, not all **archaeologists** are trained as scientists and they may not describe themselves as scientists.

Another branch that could be included here is metallurgy which is the study of **metals** and their **properties**. Metallurgists are interested in the methods used in extracting metals from their ores, purifying metals and making **alloys**, and creating useful objects from metals.

Health is listed as a single branch of science but could be broken down into other branches depending on the specialist work that people do. For example, doctors and nurses use different knowledge and skills from a radiographer who takes X-rays to show bones and other **organs** inside the body. A medical laboratory technologist uses different knowledge and skills again, working in a pathology laboratory testing blood and urine and carrying out other tests.

Scientists find out about the past

The example of early agriculture from the Kuk swamp in the Western Highlands is important because it shows two different examples of the use of science. Firstly, it shows that thousands of years ago people in Papua New Guinea used their **traditional knowledge** to grow crops and make wooden tools to dig drainage channels. This is one of the earliest examples of agriculture anywhere in the world which shows that they had a well developed understanding of crops and how to grow them. Secondly, it shows that archaeologists can use scientific processes to find out about the past.

Doing a fair experiment

Most young people have very well developed ideas of what it means to be fair and students should have no problem understanding the concept of fairness as it applies to their own lives. For example, when playing games and sport students know that it is fair to have different divisions for boys and girls and for different age groups and to have a number of rounds or heats and a final to find the best team or players. If there is a running track nearby that the students can visit, they could try the **staggered start** used for longer races which shows the idea of fairness very well, but a running track is not needed to have a good understanding of fairness.

Students also usually know when another player is cheating and when a decision is made that is not fair. However, some students may have difficulty understanding that a decision against them can still be fair. They also understand about fairness and cheating when they are taking a test for assessment. The examples from sport and everyday life can lead to the idea of being fair when conducting experiments in science.

The idea of having a test and control is one of the most important ideas in science and teachers need to make sure students get a good understanding of this principle. The example of two groups of students designing and carrying out their own experiment shows this importance in a way that students should be able to understand.

Teachers should discuss this with students to make sure that they have a clear understanding.

The idea of being able to repeat experiments is also important. When an experiment is repeated and similar results are obtained each time then we can feel more confident that we are using the scientific method properly.

When we carry out fair experiments the information that we obtain is more likely to be reliable. This means that the information is more likely to be honest and true so that we can believe it.

Cause and effect

Students may not know the expression 'cause and effect' but they do know that things happen for a reason. Scientists are always interested in the reason why things happen so that they can better understand. The example that is used to explain this is the **rain shadow**. Although most parts of Papua New Guinea usually have good rain throughout the year some places have a distinct dry **season** because they are in a rain shadow. For example, Port Moresby, the Markham Valley and parts of Milne Bay lie in a rain shadow and experience a regular dry season when little rain falls for many months of the year. At the same time there may be heavy rain at a place that is only a few kilometres away. For example, Alotau in Milne Bay usually has regular rain throughout the year but Dogura, which is on the north coast on the other side of the Owen Stanley Ranges, has a long dry season with little rainfall.

However, we have to be cautious when we try to understand cause and effect. Just because two things happen at the same time does not necessarily mean that one causes the other.

Steps in doing experiments

Teachers should discuss the three steps in doing experiments—making observations, making an inference and making a hypothesis. Students may have difficulty with the difference between an inference and a hypothesis but the examples that are linked to observations should help to make the distinction clear.

Science in the community

Science is important because it can help us to understand the world and to improve the way that we live in the community. When people have reliable information and a good understanding of how and why things happen in the world then they are better able to make good decisions and choices about the way that they live and the way they use the environment. Again, this should not be taught just as a separate topic but teachers should integrate various examples throughout the course. Many examples have been included in the student book and teachers should add to these depending on the local situation.

Equipment needed for the activities and investigations

To complete the investigations in this chapter each group of students will need the following.

For you to try (page 5)

1 Old newspapers for the students to cut out articles.

For you to try (page 9)

3 Students need to be able to visit a running or athletics track so they can see how a staggered start works.

For you to try (page 13)

2 Box of matches and a candle.

3 A thin candle and a thick candle, a ruler and some string or similar equipment to make a simple balance.

4 Two mugs or cups that are exactly the same and a saucer, or two identical mugs that have their own lids (these are often sold in trade stores).

5 Three cups or mugs (which are exactly the same), tea, coffee, or Milo, milk or sugar, cold water in dish or bucket.

Answers and explanations

For you to try (page 5)

1 Answers will vary depending on the students and their range of experience. Examples could come from the time they were babies or young children or from things they have learnt very recently.

For you to try (page 5)

1 The way that students achieve this activity will depend on them being able to find suitable articles in old newspapers. They may need help in explaining why knowledge of science would be helpful in understanding the article.

For you to try (page 7)

1 **a** People were digging drainage ditches so that they could start a new tea plantation.
b They found some very old wooden paddles or spades that were used to dig drains and they also found the remains of some old drainage ditches.
c They found the remains of layers of drains at different levels, with the lowest drains being the oldest. They found out that taro was being grown about 10 000 years ago and that people started growing banana about 7000 years ago. They also found volcanic ash which showed that there had been twenty volcanic eruptions in the area.
d The archaeologists concluded that the Western Highlands is one of the first places where people started to grow food crops. Growing food in this part of Papua New Guinea is one of the oldest examples of agriculture anywhere in the world.

For you to try (page 9)

1 Answers will vary but groups are likely to come up with rules such as the following:
- There will be separate events for boys and girls.
- There will be separate events for different age groups.
- The distance will be 100 metres. The start line and the finish line will be marked by a line of sand on the grass. There will be no **lanes** but runners will be spread out across the start line and one runner must not run in front of another.
- There will be heats every week for four weeks and the best runners will take part in the finals at the end of four weeks.
- An umpire (or umpires) will be chosen to make sure that the runners follow the rules.
- A runner who does not follow the rules will be given one warning. A runner who does not follow the rules a second time will be disqualified from the competition.

2 For races of 200 metres or longer a staggered start is used on an athletics track because for these longer races the curved part of the track must be used. The inside part of the curve is shorter than the outside which would not be fair to all runners. To compensate for this the runner on the inside starts further back and the runner on the outside track starts furthest forward. The other runners are spaced out equally in between the inside and outside runner. All runners cross the same finishing line and by the end of the race they have all run the same distance, if the track has been set out properly.

3 If students are able to visit a running or athletics track and try a few simple experiments they should find that it does not make any difference if a runner is on the inside lane or the outside lane. If they do find a consistent difference between the lanes then it may mean that the track has not been measured and set out properly. A special wheel is used to measure distances on the ground since it is difficult to use a tape measure for long distances and for curves.

Even though the distance for each runner may be the same, some runners may find that they prefer one lane to the other. For example, on the curved part of the track the runner on the inside lane can see all the other runners in front of him or her, but the runner in the outside lane will not be able to see any of the other runners because they will be behind.

4 Answers will vary but groups are likely to come up with reasons such as the following:
- Different age groups or levels of ability.
- Different numbers of players on each side or team.
- One person or team having different or better equipment than the others.
- One person or team being given more time than the others.
- One person or team playing very aggressively.
- One person or team not following the rules.
- The umpire applying the rules very strictly to one person or team but not to others.
- Some people or teams may play better at different times of the day than others.
- Some people or teams may play better in different kinds of weather.
- The wind may help some players more than others.
- Some people believe that there is an advantage for a person or team playing at home compared to when they play away from home, especially when there are lots of encouraging supporters who are shouting and cheering.

5 A referee or umpire can help to make a game fair by having a good knowledge and understanding of the rules of the game. The referee or umpire must then apply the rules fairly and consistently to all players and not favour particular players over the others. The referee or umpire will need to make quick decisions and communicate them to the players. Because it is difficult for a referee or umpire to see what is happening in all parts of the sports field he or she may be assisted by one or more linesman or judge to help decide if the ball has crossed the line.

For you to try (page 12)

1 When you carried out your experiment you were trying to find out if stirring helps sugar to dissolve faster in water. You stirred both containers in the same way but you also changed the temperature of the water. In your result you found that the sugar dissolved more quickly in the container with warm water than the one with cold water. You concluded that the difference in the results was due to stirring. This conclusion does not follow from your result. Although stirring may have helped the sugar to dissolve, in your case the difference in temperature is helping the sugar to dissolve. If you stirred both containers in exactly the same way then the difference in the result must be due to the temperature not the stirring. In order to find out about stirring you need to keep the temperature of the water the same, but change the amount of stirring in different containers.

For you to try (page 13)

1 Answers will vary but some different inferences or possible conclusions from the observations are as follows:
- Smelling onions in the kitchen.
  - ➢ Onions are now on sale in the local store.
  - ➢ Your mother has been to the store to buy onions.
  - ➢ Somebody is preparing food for a party.
- Finding that some new material feels smooth and silky.
  - ➢ The material must be man-made or synthetic material.
  - ➢ The material will feel hot and sticky next to the skin.
  - ➢ The material will melt when heated and drip when it burns.
- Seeing a boy running away.
  - ➢ The boy has done something wrong.
  - ➢ The boy has just remembered that he has something important to do.
  - ➢ The boy thinks that it is going rain heavily and wants to find shelter.
- Hearing a chicken make a lot of noise.
  - ➢ The chicken is being chased by a dog or by some children.

- ➢ Someone is trying to catch the chicken to kill it and cook it.
- ➢ The chicken is hungry and wants some food.
- Tasting a lemon and finding that it is sour.
  - ➢ All lemons have a sour taste.
  - ➢ Lemons are not good for eating.
  - ➢ If lemon juice was squeezed on to fish it would taste good.

2 Investigation: Observing a burning candle

Answers will vary but may include the following:

Observation	Inference
The main part of the flame is yellow.	The flame would leave a dirty mark on something that was placed in the flame.
Sometimes the **liquid** wax runs down the side of the candle.	The wax runs down the side when more wax melts than is being burned by the wick.
The centre part of the flame is a different colour to the outside part—more blue.	One part of the flame is hotter than another part.
The burning flame produces a smell.	The wax contains some sort of perfume.
The top part of the wick is black but the lower part is white.	The **molten** wax stops the wick from burning.
The flame moves in the wind.	The flame is a kind of **gas**.
When the candle is alight the wax around the wick melts.	Heat makes the wax change from a **solid** to a liquid.
When the liquid wax runs down the outside of the candle it changes back to a solid.	Cooling is needed to make the liquid wax change back to a solid again.
The candle will not light if the wick is too short.	The liquid wax must be able to move up the wick.

3 Investigation: Thin candles and thick candles

Very thin candles like those that we put on a birthday cake do burn down more quickly than a thick candle like the ones that are sometimes used in church. Birthday cake candles are made to be used once only and to last for a very short time—just long enough for people to sing 'Happy birthday' and then be blown out. The thick candles that are used in churches will last for many weeks even though they are lit every Sunday and burn for the whole service.

In order to find out if more wax is burned in one candle than in another we need to begin with a hypothesis which could be like one of the following:

- 'that thin candles use up more wax than thick candles when they burn' or
- 'that thick candles use up more wax than thin candles when they burn' or
- 'that there is no difference in the amount of wax that is used up by thick and thin candles when they burn'.

The next step is to compare the **mass** of the candles. This can be done using a simple balance which the students can make.

Using this equipment it is likely that the students will find that there is no difference that they can measure in the amount of wax that is used up in thick and thin candles. If the wick is the same size in both candles then the amount of wax used up will be the same and will not depend on the width of the candle. However, if the wick is thicker then it may use up more wax.

4 **Investigation: Does a lid keep a drink hot for longer?**
In this investigation students need to put the same amount of the same hot drink in two identical cups. The control cup should be left without a lid and the test cup should have its own lid or a saucer. Students should find that the drink stays hot for longer in the cup with the lid than in the cup without the lid. They should be able to tell the difference by feeling the outside of the cup and by tasting a small amount of the drink. It would be more accurate to use a thermometer to measure the temperature, but it is still possible to get a clear result without a thermometer.

5 **Investigation: Can you make a hot drink cool down more quickly by pouring it into a cold cup?**
In this investigation both cups A and B must be exactly the same and the amount of drink and type of drink must also be the same. The only thing that is changed is the way that the drink cools down.

The drink in cup A will cool down slowly and remain hot for longer. The drink in cup B will cool down more quickly because each time it is poured into a cold cup some of the heat from the drink is used to heat up the cup. The heat is conducted from the hot drink to the cold cup and so the drink cools down.

For you to try (page 15)

1 Students will come up with different ideas in their discussion and these might be based on the list of bullet points in the student book or other ideas.

2 Science can help people to make responsible choices to improve community life as follows:
- Knowing how to grow and prepare good food and eat a healthy diet and avoiding food that is not nutritious or can lead to sickness, for example, foods that contain too much fat or sugar.
- Knowing how to prevent sickness and knowing what to do when we get sick, for example, keeping our bodies, homes and the community clean.
- Preventing pests like rats, cockroaches, flies and mosquitoes from reproducing easily, so that they do not spread diseases.
- Understanding the reasons for building and using proper toilets such as pit toilets in order to stay healthy.
- Avoiding activities that can make us sick like smoking, chewing betel nut, drinking too much alcohol and using marijuana.
- Being careful about sexual behaviour so that we do not catch a sexually transmissible disease or have unwanted pregnancies.
- By making good decisions about the way that we use **resources** from the environment, for example, fishing, **logging** and mining.
- Understanding different ways of getting rid of rubbish and using these in the community to prevent sickness.

Projects

1 **Making hot food go cold**
We can make a saucepan of hot food go cold quickly by:
- standing it in a bowl of cold water and changing the water when it gets warm
- wrapping the saucepan in cloth and keeping the cloth damp with cold water
- placing the saucepan in front of a fan
- placing the saucepan in a refrigerator (although a very hot saucepan should be allowed to cool a little before being placed in a refrigerator).

In order to test each of these ideas we need two identical saucepans each with the same amount of hot food inside. The control saucepan should be allowed to cool down naturally and not given any treatment. The test saucepan should be given one of the treatments listed above. It should be possible to feel the difference in temperature, although a thermometer would give a more accurate result.

2 Using science to make life better

Students will come up with different ideas but the list of bullet points under 'For you to try' (2), page 21, may also help to provide further possible projects.

Summary questions

1

Science is	T or F?
a way of doing things	T
a way of looking at things	T
a way of thinking about things	T

2 A

3

Steps in the scientific method	Order
A asking a question that guides our observations	1
B suggesting a possible answer to the question	2
C testing the ideas by doing an experiment	3
D recording the results of the experiment	4
E checking if the results support the possible answer that was suggested before	5
F thinking again and carrying out more experiments if needed	6
G making final conclusions	7

4 C

5

When an experiment is fair …	T or F?
somebody else should also be able to repeat the experiment and get the same results	T
if different people repeat the same experiment and get a different result we can feel more confident about our experiments	F
repeating the experiment can help to understand why something is happening and that nothing is being missed	T

6

Word	Meaning	Answer
A control	**1** something that you notice with your senses	E
B hypothesis	**2** an experiment or project that you do to answer a question	D
C inference	**3** a comparison so that a fair experiment is done	A
D investigation	**4** an explanation of what you observed	C
E observation	**5** a guess at an answer that you can check by experiment	B

7 When we want to find out about something and understand it better, we often carry out **experiments** or investigations. Investigations often start with a **question** or a problem, we choose a **method** in order to get some results and then we make a **conclusion**. This way of doing things is called the **scientific** method. When we are planning an investigation we must make sure that it is **fair** in order to find out why things happen and how they work. We often have to make and use simple **equipment** in order to collect information that will help us to carry out investigations. When we have collected **information** we can use it to make and support a conclusion. After carrying out an investigation we should **decide** whether it was a fair test. Science can be used to **improve** community life by making sure we make responsible **choices** that are based on reliable information.

STRAND 2 Living things

About this strand

This strand further develops the ideas introduced in Grade 6 on the nature of living things and the relationships between living things. It consists of two sub-strands. The first sub-strand **Nature of living things** begins by looking at the way in which we can classify plants into five main groups and the **adaptations** they have made that help them live successfully in different environments; for example, **roots** and **shoots**. Students will then look at ways of classifying animals into those with backbones or **vertebrates** and those without backbones or **invertebrates**. Students will learn how to use a key to sort animals with backbones into five main groups. In particular students look at the body coverings of animals and the way in which these coverings are suited to the environment in which the animal lives. Students will collect information from their own observations and make conclusions about the way in which the structure is related to the function or the job that it does. Students go on to look at adaptations for feeding in animals, particularly the mouth parts of insects, birds and **mammals**. The ideas about feeding are developed to look at the way that the **digestive system** works in different vertebrates.

The second sub-strand again looks at **Ecology, relationships and interactions** between **organisms** in the environment. Students will find out more about the importance of feeding relationships by looking at **food chains** and constructing **food webs**. Food chains are further explored by looking at the pyramid of numbers and the pyramid of **biomass** to explain the transfer of **energy** through a food chain. Students will also find out about the **predator–prey** relationship and competition between living things. Finally, students will discuss the ways in which the lessons we learn from **ecology** can help to manage the environment wisely.

Sub-strands 1 and 2

Main ideas

Sub-strand 1: Plants and animals have different structures and adaptations that allow them to function successfully in their environment.

Sub-strand 2: The living things in a community of plants and animals, including humans, are in a relationship called a food web. The lessons that we learn from ecology can be used to help manage the environment wisely.

Key words

Adaptations, variation, invertebrate, vertebrate, **monotreme**, **marsupial**, **placental**, **camouflage**, cartilaginous, **carnivore**, **herbivore**, **omnivore**, digestive system, **digestion**, **elimination**, **ruminant**, ecology, **habitat**, community, **ecosystem**, **producer**, **consumer**, food chain, food web, **decomposer**, **biodegradable**, pyramid of numbers, pyramid of biomass, predator, prey, competition, **diverse**, **fertiliser**, **pesticide**.

Key facts

- The structure of living things helps them to live in the environment.
- The different structures of living things allow them to live in different environments.
- The structure of the different parts of living things is related to the job which the part must carry out.
- All animals have a body covering that is suited to the place where it lives.
- The digestive system of humans allows us to break down food that we eat.
- Breaking down food provides us with energy and also produces waste.
- Other animals also have a digestive system. The type of digestive system depends on the kind of food that the animal eats.
- The plants and animals living together in an ecosystem are in a feeding relationship called a food web.
- Human beings are also part of a food web and have a relationship with plants and other animals in the environment.
- The activities of humans have a bigger impact on the environment than any other animal because of the way we obtain food and use other resources.

Assessment tasks

Assessment aims to gather information on how well students have achieved the outcomes of the strand. A variety of strategies should be used: practical, written and oral.

Each assessment item should be based on criteria that have been clearly written down. Students should be told what the criteria are so that they know the basis for judgment of their achievement and demonstration of the outcomes.

Assessment should also be continuous and collected throughout the learning process by the completion of appropriate activities such as those indicated with the assessment icon in the 'For you to try' sections.

Major links to other subjects

Strand 2: Living things builds on ideas introduced in Culture and Community at the elementary level and Environmental Studies at the lower primary level. At the upper primary level, **Living things** links to the strand Health of Individuals and Population in Personal Development. Aspects of different subjects can be integrated into activities such as:

- a project to improve life in the community
- collecting and analysing statistical data for specific groups in the community
- designing posters or performing a drama to relay the message of the benefits of using the methods of science.

Links with other subjects are noted with an icon in the student books.

Teacher information

Sorting out plants

This chapter begins by building on the ideas that were introduced in Grade 6 on the **classification** of living things.

The five main groups that scientists use to classify plants are introduced but teachers could discuss the reasons why most people can classify garden plants into the main groups of:

- fruits and vegetables
- flowers and weeds.

Teachers could also ask students about traditional ways of sorting plants into groups.

A more detailed classification of plants is included below, moving from the simple **algae** to the more complex **conifers** and flowering plants. **Fungi** are listed here for the sake of completeness although they have no **chlorophyll** and so cannot make their own food. Fungi are not described as a group in the student book, only their role as decomposers.

Algae

- Algae are classified as simple water plants. They all live in wet or damp conditions.
- Algae do not have roots, leaves, **stems** or flowers.
- Algae attach by holdfasts or are free floating.
- Algae vary in size from microscopic to giant kelps that may grow to 50 metres in length.
- Algae may have many different colours; for example, red and brown seaweed.
- Algae are a major source of food for animals that live in the water. Free-living microscopic algae are called plant **plankton** and are a basic food source.
- Algae are classed as producers because they make their own food.

Mosses and liverworts

- **Mosses** and **liverworts** are the smallest simple green land plants.
- All mosses and liverworts are smaller than 50 centimetres and most mosses are less than two centimetres in height.
- Most mosses and liverworts live in damp places and where it is cool.
- Mosses and liverworts do not have true roots, stems or leaves although they have similar structures.
- Mosses and liverworts have thread-like structures called rhizoids that allow them to hold on to tree trunks and rocks.
- Mosses and liverworts reproduce by spores and can also reproduce asexually.
- Mosses and liverworts have two parts to their life cycle.
- Mosses and liverworts help to break down plant material and rocks.

Ferns

- **Ferns** are classified as higher plants because of their many specialised **cells**.
- Ferns vary in size from less than two centimetres across to tree ferns that can grow up to ten metres tall.
- Ferns have well-developed transport systems.
- Ferns have roots, stems and leaves.
- The leaves of ferns are called fronds.
- Ferns have no flowers. They reproduce by spores that form on the back of the fronds.
- Ferns may reproduce asexually from the stem.
- Ferns have two stages in their life cycle.
- Some ferns are poisonous and need to be destroyed; for example, bracken ferns are poisonous to pigs; salvinia can block rivers and lakes.
- Some ferns are edible and used for food.

Conifers and flowering plants

- Conifers and flowering plants have specialised cells.
- Transport systems carry materials within conifers and flowering plants.
- The major difference between the two groups is in methods of reproduction:
  - ➢ Conifers have exposed seeds formed in cones.
  - ➢ Flowering plants have enclosed seeds formed within a fruit. This develops from the flower.

- Conifers and flowering plants have a wide number of uses. They provide food and many materials that people use every day.
- The trees in the rain forest are flowering plants.
- The four main types of forest in Papua New Guinea are:
  - ➢ Lowland rain forests
  - ➢ Low mountain forests
  - ➢ Mid-mountain forests
  - ➢ High mountain forests.

Fungi

- Fungi are plants in some ways but have no chlorophyll and so they cannot make their own food.
- Fungi usually live on dead remains of other plants or animals.
- Fungi vary in size from microscopic yeasts to large mushrooms.
- Fungi have no true roots and a poor internal transport system.
- Fungi reproduce by spores. The spores grow when moisture and warmth are present.
- Some fungi are used for food; for example:
  - ➢ edible mushrooms (many mushrooms are poisonous)
  - ➢ yeast which is used to make bread and beer
  - ➢ a special fungus is used to make the medicine penicillin
  - ➢ a fungus can be used to make special cheeses known as blue cheese.
- The most important use of fungi is breaking down dead material as decomposers.
- Fungi and algae together can form a plant called a lichen which is often the first plant to grow on bare rock. For this reason lichens are sometimes called pioneer plants.

The structure of flowering plants

For the **Investigation: Looking at different plants** make sure that the plants are numbered so that everyone can look at the same set and compare their results.

Throughout this first topic teachers should stress that it is the adaptations of plants, particularly shoots and roots, that enable them to be successful in a range of environments.

Teachers may have to further explain the concept of variation to students and be prepared to give examples to support this.

Sorting out animals

The classification of animals is complex and at the upper primary level students should not be expected to learn all the groups or difficult scientific names. However, the table below will help the teacher appreciate the level of complexity of different groups of animals and know their names. The simplest animals are at the top of the list and the level of complexity increases down the list.

The main groups of animals

Type of animal	Example	Scientific group
Single celled	Amoeba	Protozoa
Sponges	Cup sponge	Porifera
Hollow bodies and stinging cells	Jellyfish	Coelenterates
Flatworms	Tapeworm	Platyhelminthes
Roundworms	Hookworm	Nematodes
Spiny skinned	Sea urchin	Echinoderms
Shellfish	Oyster	Molluscs
Segmented worms	Earthworm	Annelids
External **skeleton** with jointed legs	Crab	Arthropods
Internal skeleton with backbone	Snake	Vertebrates

This topic concentrates mainly on the five main groups of vertebrates. Although monotremes, marsupials and placentals are introduced as three sub-groups of mammals, teachers should not place too much emphasis on students learning these terms.

For you to try (pages 35, 37)

In the **Investigations: Looking at a lizard** and **Observing a frog** in which students collect and observe live animals, teachers should teach and encourage the concept of respect for life. Animals should be released unharmed when students have finished their investigation.

Sorting out vertebrates

The use of keys to classify living things was introduced in Grade 6 but some students may still need help in using them. To use the key, start at the top and read across the table from left to right. Start with number 1 and choose 'a' or 'b'. After you have answered the first pair of questions you must then answer the next pair of questions, if appropriate, and so on. Continue until you have sorted the unknown animals into one of the five groups.

As an extension activity for students who like a challenge teachers could get them to design their own key to classify a group of living things or other objects. The important feature of a key is that each pair of questions must have a clear 'yes' or 'no' answer and should divide the objects progressively until they have been classified into groups. Students can try out their keys on each other and should be prepared to modify them if questions are not clear or if the key does not work properly.

Adaptations for feeding

Teachers should again stress that it is the adaptations of animals that enable them to be successful in a range of environments. For example, insects are one of the most successful groups of animals and about three-quarters of the total number of animals in the world are insects.

The examples in the student book concentrate on mouthparts as adaptations for feeding although animals have many other adaptations. Students begin by finding out about insect mouthparts, then bird beaks and finally the teeth of mammals. This topic concludes by looking at the care of teeth and teachers should emphasise the steps that students can take to keep their teeth healthy.

The digestive system

Students who have not seen pigs being cut up may be surprised at the length of the digestive tube. Teachers could also discuss how the length of the digestive system, together with the internal structures, helps increase the surface area for digestion and therefore, the absorption of digested food.

What happens after digestion?

The table that shows what happens to food after digestion is included in the student book but students should not be expected to remember the names of different digestive juices or **enzymes**.

Ecology, relationships and interactions

The main purpose of this sub-strand is to further develop the basic ideas in ecology that were introduced in Grade 6 about the way in which plants and animals interact in the environment.

Feeding is the most important relationship and the concepts of producer, herbivore, carnivore and omnivore were introduced in Grade 6. Students now find out about decomposers and biodegradable materials.

Students should understand the concept of the food chain and food web. The pyramid of numbers was introduced in Grade 6 and now the pyramid of biomass is introduced.

Points for discussion when looking at food chains and food webs.

- The organisms in an ecosystem can be divided into producers and consumers.
- There are also different levels of consumers depending on their position in the food chain.
- The first organism in a food chain is always a plant or producer.
- The second organism in the food chain is a consumer. It is also a herbivore because it consumes plants.
- The third organism in the food chain is a consumer. It is usually a carnivore because it consumes animals. Organisms in this group are also known as lower carnivores.
- The fourth organism in a food chain is a consumer. It is usually a carnivore because it consumes animals. Organisms in this group are also known as higher level carnivores.
- Food chains do not usually contain more than four organisms (although **scavengers** may be the fifth organism).

Pyramid of numbers and Pyramid of biomass

Students will need to be able to perform simple calculations in order to complete this topic.

Changing populations

The ideas of predator and prey are introduced and the predator–prey relationship.

Using our environment wisely

This chapter ends by looking at the lessons that we can learn from ecology to help manage the environment wisely. The examples used include logging and the use of chemical fertilisers and pesticides. Other examples that the teacher could mention are fishing and the problems of introduced species like the cane toad, water hyacinth and salvinia. These ideas are developed further in Grade 8, in both chapter one and chapter two of the student book.

Equipment needed for the activities and investigations

To complete the activities and investigations in this chapter each group of students will need the following.

For you to try (page 23)
Investigation: Finding the height of a tree

- A metre ruler and a measuring tape. Students will also need to find a tree in a place where they can easily and safely measure the shadow of the tree. They will also need a sunny day. If students do not have a measuring tape, then they can use a piece of string to find the length of the shadow of the ruler and see how many times this fits into the length of the shadow of the tree. The answer will be the height of the tree in metres.

For you to try (page 27)
Investigation: Looking at different plants

- Each group should collect a number or different types of plants. A magnifying glass would also be useful.

Project: Growing native trees

- Collect seeds from native trees that grow in your area or another area, and pots or containers with holes for drainage and some soil. A place will also be needed as a nursery where the seedlings can be cared for. The seedlings may also need some shade when they first start to grow.

Answers and explanations

For you to try (page 27)

2 **a** Conifers have seeds in cones, roots, a woody stem, but no flowers.
b Algae have no true roots, stems or leaves.
c Mosses have no stem, simple roots and no leaves.
d Flowering plants have seeds, roots, stems and flowers.
e Conifers, ferns, mosses and algae are all non-flowering plants.
f Flowering plants and conifers both produce seeds. Flowering plants have broad leaves and produce flowers that can develop into seeds inside the fruit. Conifers have narrow leaves shaped like a needle and produce male and female cones instead of flowers.
g The stem is the structure that allows ferns to grow much taller than mosses.
h Pond slime that you find on a rock is an alga and does not have roots, stems or leaves. A moss has structures that look like roots, stems and leaves although these are not true roots, stems and leaves.

i Conifers have two types of cones that are needed for reproduction. The male cone produces pollen and the female cone produces seeds.

For you to try (page 31)

1 The cassowary is suited or adapted to the environment in the following ways:
- Although it cannot fly it has strong legs for walking and scratching the ground.
- It has large claws that it can use to defend itself since it cannot fly away.
- It has a bony plate on the top of its head which can be used to push through the bush.

2 When birds mark their **territory** by singing it is helpful because it means that other birds will keep away which reduces the competition. It is usually better for a bird to try to find its own territory than risk being attacked by entering the territory of another bird. Each bird needs an area that is big enough to supply its needs. Having territories also helps to disperse the birds so they spread out over a larger area. This helps the species to survive because if birds in one area die due to some unusual event then those from a distant area where conditions are different may be able to survive. The area where birds died may then be able to be repopulated later.

Living things

For you to try (page 32)

1 Characteristics that mammals have in common are:
- fur or hair on the body
- two pairs of limbs
- they are warm blooded and most have sweat glands to help them cool down
- lungs to breathe.

2 Marsupials like the wallaby are different from other mammals because the young are born when they are very small and not well developed. They crawl to the pouch of the mother where they develop. They are able to feed on milk while they are in the pouch.

3

Dolphins and whales	
Similarities with fish	**Characteristics shared with mammals**
Live in water	Warm blooded
Shape and structure of body is like a fish	Have lungs for breathing
Swim using the tail	Young are born live
	Young feed on mother's milk
	Parents take care of the young

4 Examples of herbivores are cuscus, wallaby, bandicoot, dugong, horse, goat, sheep, and cow.

5 Students will choose a variety of different mammals so answers will vary. However, an example of how a dugong or sea cow is adapted to live in its environment is shown below:
- It has a **streamlined** shape that is suitable for swimming in the sea.
- The tail moves up and down to make the animal move through the water.
- The fore-limbs are like paddles that help it move and feed more easily.
- The mouth is turned down so that it can pull up and feed on seagrasses.
- It has the teeth of a herbivore, especially the **incisors**, for eating grasses (this is the reason it is also known as the sea cow).
- It has heavy bones, among the heaviest in the animal kingdom, that act as ballast and allow the dugong to remain suspended just below the surface of the water.
- The body is covered with short hair that scientists think may allow it to feel the environment more easily.

For you to try (page 36)

1 Four types of **reptiles** are the crocodile, lizard, turtle and snake.
   - Crocodiles can live in salt water or fresh water. They can swim and dive under water using their powerful tail. They also have four legs and so can walk on the land. The legs do not lift the body far off the ground but each leg swings round before it to make the crocodile move forward.
   - Lizards usually live on the land in a variety of different places and have four legs that enable them to walk. Some lizards can climb trees and geckoes are able to climb walls and walk upside down under the roof or on the ceiling. Many lizards are also able to swim.
   - Turtles like those found in Papua New Guinea usually live in the sea but must come out to a beach in order to lay their eggs. They have four limbs that can be used as paddles when swimming in the sea. When the turtle lands on a beach the limbs are used to drag the animal over the sand. Turtles found in Papua New Guinea are not able to support their own **weight** on their legs alone, but some turtles can do this.
   - Snakes can live in a wide variety of environments and are found in many parts of Papua New Guinea. Snakes do not have legs but are able to move forwards by changing the shape of the body. Snakes have scales on the outside that help them to grip as they move. Snakes can move along the ground and some are also able to climb. Some snakes can swim in rivers and lakes and some will swim in the sea.

2 A gecko can walk up walls and walk upside down on the roof or ceiling because it has special **friction** pads on its feet that enable it to grip.

3 Answers will vary depending on the area, but crocodile and turtle are eaten in some parts of Papua New Guinea, although it may only be on special occasions. Lizards and snakes may also be eaten—both are eaten in other parts of the world.

4 Rules for staying safe where there are snakes.
   - If you think there are snakes where you are walking, stamp on the ground as you walk so that they can hear you coming and then they will usually keep away from you.
   - When it is cool watch out for snakes on the road or other open spaces where they may be warming themselves.
   - Do not try to catch snakes or play with them because you are more likely to be bitten.
   - If you are bitten by a snake you should visit the nearest health worker, if possible.

   Answers will vary but snakes may be seen more commonly when it is cooler and they are warming themselves in the open, such as on a rock or on a road.

For you to try (page 37)

2
   - **Amphibians** like the frog are adapted to their environment in a number of ways. They can breathe in different ways depending on their stage in the life cycle. Adults have lungs and moist skin so they can breathe through the lungs when they are in water as well as through the skin when they are on land.
   - Many amphibians need to return to water in order to reproduce. The water is used to carry the sperm to the egg which is protected by jelly that surrounds the egg.
   - The eggs grow into tadpoles that breathe using **gills** and then develop into young frogs that breathe using lungs. After lungs have developed the young frog can move out of the water. However, many of the frogs in Papua New Guinea do not need to return to water in order to reproduce. Because it is usually wet in the rain forest, eggs can be laid in damp moss or leaf litter and so when they hatch, these eggs do not go through a tadpole stage.
   - Amphibians also have different ways of feeding depending on the stage in the life cycle. For example, tadpoles feed on water plants, but most adults feed on insects and worms. The adult frogs have sticky tongues that move in and out very quickly and can be used to catch food.

For you to try (page 39)

1 Examples will vary but some possible responses are shown below.

Animal group and example	Body covering	How is the body covering suited to the environment?
Birds e.g. wagtail	Feathers	Feathers are light and so help the bird to fly. Feathers trap air and so help to keep the bird warm. The colours of the feathers may also be used for camouflage to protect the bird or to attract a mate.
Mammals e.g. cuscus	Fur or hair	Fur helps the cuscus to keep warm and protects the skin from being cut or broken.
Fish e.g. barramundi	Scales	Scales allow the fish to move easily through the water and also help to protect the fish.
Reptile e.g. turtle	Dry skin and shell	The shell protects the turtle against predators and the skin is tough, like leather.
Amphibian e.g. frog	Moist skin	Skin protects the frog and also allows the frog to breathe on land because it is moist.
Invertebrate e.g. crab, crayfish	Hard shell or exoskeleton	The hard shell protects the crab or crayfish against predators. Spines or nails may also provide further protection.

2 The student sorted six living things into those that do not have wings and so cannot fly (Group A) and those that have wings and can fly (Group B).

3

- Snakes and worms both have a similar shape and neither of them has legs. They are both able to move in one direction by changing the shape of the body. Both have a body covering that allows them to grip so that they can move. Both usually live on the land.
- They are placed in different groups because the snake has a backbone and so is a vertebrate, whereas the worm does not have a backbone and so is an invertebrate.

4 One method for sorting the following living things into three separate groups is as follows:

Animals that can swim	Animals that can fly	Animals that cannot fly
barramundi, salmon, seal, trout, shark, tuna	crow, eagle, flying fox	cat, dog, elephant, goat, horse, pig, possum, wallaby, whale

For you to try (page 44)

1

- Eat a good diet that includes milk, cheese and beans that all contain calcium.
- Do not eat sweet foods between meals.
- Do not drink sweet drinks like fizzy soft drinks because it leads to tooth decay.
- Brush your teeth at least once per day. Good toothpaste contains fluoride and the best time is after eating a meal and before you go to bed.
- Brush your teeth firmly for three to four minutes each time. Make sure that all parts of the teeth are brushed. Move the brush up and down so that the bristles go into the space between the teeth and the gums.
- Do not chew betel nut and lime, which damage the teeth and the gums and may cause the teeth to fall out.
- Do not open bottles using your teeth because it can damage them.
- Visit the dentist regularly so that any tooth decay or gum disease can be treated.

2

- Carnivores like dogs eat meat and have incisors for gripping and large **canines** for holding and tearing their food. They have **premolars** and **molars** for cutting off flesh and cracking bones.
- Herbivores like cows eat plants and do not have canines but have a space in this part of the mouth instead. They have sharp incisors for cutting plants and molars and premolars with sharp ridges on the surfaces. These teeth are needed for crushing plant cells and chewing because the plant cell wall is made of a tough substance called **cellulose**.
- Omnivores like humans eat both meat and plants. The incisors and canines are similar and are used for biting off pieces of food. The molars and premolars are used for grinding food.

For you to try (page 50)

1

- A producer is a plant that is able to make its own food by the process of **photosynthesis**. All green plants use chlorophyll to change the energy of the sun into food energy, for example, grass.
- A consumer is an animal that eats food because it is not able to make its own. Some consumers eat plants and some consumers eat other animals, for example, mosquitoes.

2 Biodegradable materials are things that can rot or decompose because of the action of microbes such as bacteria and fungi; for example, food and wood.

3 Waste that is biodegradable such as food scraps can be fed to animals or put on a compost heap and later put on the garden. Timber and pieces of wood may be used again or burned as firewood. Paper and cardboard can often be used more than once. Some non-biodegradable materials can be recycled. For example, plastic bags, bottles and some metals like cans can be used again. Biodegradable materials that cannot be recycled should be collected and dumped in a hole in the ground away from water sources and away from the places where people live. The rubbish should be covered with soil when there is no more space.

4 The octopus and the crab would be affected because they eat the periwinkle. The seal and the seagull would also be affected because they both eat octopus and crab.

5

Alternative names used for organisms in a food chain			
Plant	Animal	Animal	Animal
Producer	First order consumer	Second order consumer	Third order consumer
Plant	Herbivore	Carnivore	Top carnivore

For you to try (page 52)

1 a

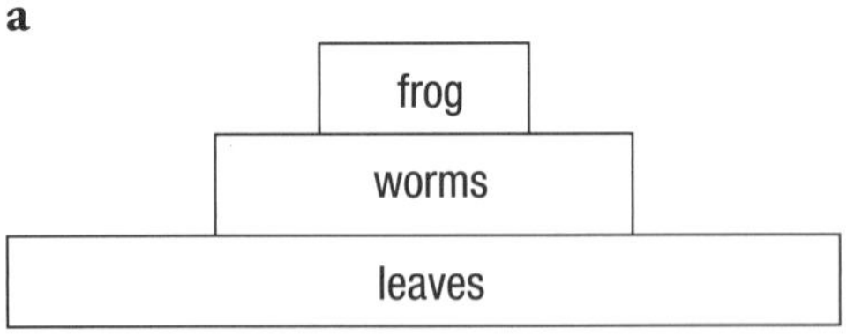

b

	A Number	B Mass of each in grams	A × B Biomass in grams
frog	1	200	200
worms	250	40	10 000
leaves	25 000	20	500 000

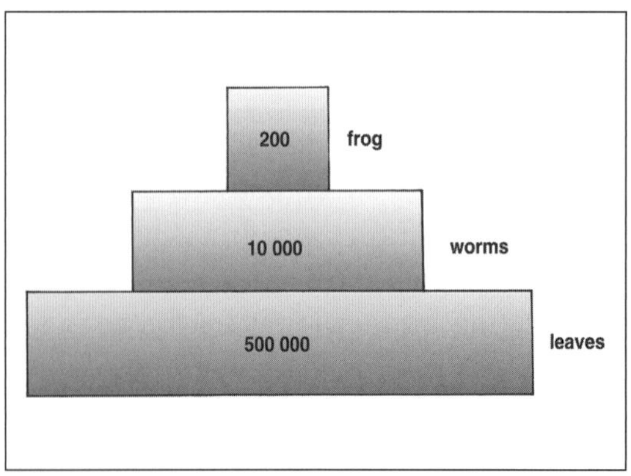

2 Groups will vary in their discussions and in the reasons they give but students may come up with some of the following:
- Growing plants to feed to animals is not efficient because so much energy is lost at each step in the food chain. The cow or pig uses this energy to live.
- It would be more efficient for humans to grow crops to eat themselves rather than to feed to animals.
- Humans need to eat protein in their diet but there are plants that are good sources of protein such as peanuts, and legumes like beans.
- The population of the world is increasing rapidly and many people do not have enough to eat. It is easier to feed people with plant foods than with expensive animal foods.
- Eating too much food from animals, especially fat, is not healthy and can make people sick.
- It is wrong to kill animals to eat.

For you to try (page 54)

1 If there are too many consumers in a food chain then they will eat so much food that it will run out and then the consumers will be hungry and may die. For this reason each level in a food chain or food pyramid can only support a smaller biomass of living things at the higher level. A balance develops between there being enough food for the level above and allowing each level to survive. Each consumer also uses up energy in order to live and this energy cannot be passed on to another consumer so energy is lost from the system.

2 **Investigation: Looking at feeding relationships**
Answers will vary depending on the local area and what students choose to look at.

Summary questions

1

		Answer
A The green material in leaves	**I** roots	I
B Plants make food in these	**II** water	G
C The largest group of plants	**III** spores	E
D Plants that have needle-like leaves and cones	**IV** chlorophyll	A
E Ferns reproduce using these	**V** flowering plants	C
F Seaweed belongs to this group of plants	**VI** leaves	B
G Needed for plants to live	**VII** photosynthesis	H
H The process in which plants make food	**VIII** mangrove	J
I Holds the plant in the ground	**IX** conifer	D
J A tree that can grow in water and has breathing roots	**X** algae	F

2 D
3 D
4 B
5 D

6

Environment in which animal lives	Body covering of animal	Answer
A Lives on the land, some can swim or dive, most can fly	**I** Dry, scaly skin of reptile	D
B Usually lives on the land producing live young	**II** Scales of fish	C
C Always lives in water	**III** Moist skin of amphibian, may be rough or smooth	E
D Usually live on land, some can live in water	**IV** Fur of mammals	B
E Can live on land or in water but usually need to be near water, especially to reproduce	**V** Feathers of birds	A

7 **a** Colobodus
b Bobasatrania
c Saurichthys

8 B
9 C
10 B
11 C
12 D
13 The structure of living things helps them to live in the **environment**. The different **structures** of living things allow them to live in different environments.

The structure of the different parts of living things is related to the **job** which the part must do. All animals have a **body** covering that is suited to the place where it lives. The **digestive** system of humans allows us to break down food that we eat.

Breaking down food provides us with **energy** and also produces waste.

Other animals also have a digestive **system**. The type of digestive system depends on the kind of **food** that the animal eats.

The plants and animals living together in an ecosystem are in a **feeding** relationship called a food web. Human beings are also part of a food web and have a **relationship** with other plants and animals in the environment. The **activities** of humans have a bigger effect on the environment than any other animal because of the way we obtain food and use other resources.

STRAND 3 Science in the home

About this strand

This strand builds on the ideas that were introduced in Grade 6 about the situations in which science is found and used in everyday life. It consists of two sub-strands. The first sub-strand **Learning about substances** looks at the structure and behaviour of **matter** in terms of the **particles** from which it is made. Students will look at the **states** of matter and be able to explain change of state using the particle model of matter. Students will find out more about the properties of materials, the way that we can classify the solids that we use, and look at the use of metals and alloys in more detail.

In order to find out more about the changes that can occur to matter, students will design and carry out simple experiments that show **physical** and **chemical changes**. The information collected will be used to explain the nature of changes in matter. For example, students will be able to explain the physical changes such as change of state, dissolving, and making and separating **mixtures**. Students will also be able to identify chemical changes, describe the energy change that takes place during a chemical reaction and write simple word equations to describe chemical changes.

In the second sub-strand **Using energy in the home** students begin by looking at heat, light and sound energy and the topic is then broadened by finding out about food energy, potential energy and **kinetic energy**. The topic continues by looking at **forces** in everyday life such as starting and stopping, speeding up and slowing down. Students find out about the four main types of forces—the force of **gravity**, magnetic forces, electrical forces and **elastic** forces. The important topic of friction is covered by looking at the causes of friction and ways of reducing friction as well as the advantages and disadvantages of friction. Finally, students find out more about simple **machines** and carry out a survey on the way simple machines are used to do work at home and make life easier for the community.

Sub-strands 1 and 2

Main ideas

Sub-strand 1: The structure and behaviour of matter can be explained by looking at the particles from which it is made. The properties of materials can change when the matter from which it is made goes through a physical change or a chemical change.

Sub-strand 2: Energy can exist in many different forms such as heat, light and sound, and can change from one form to another. Forces can be used to make things move, to slow them down and to speed them up. Simple machines can be used at home and in the community to do work.

Key words

States, matter, particles, materials, solid, liquid, gas, **strong**, **brittle**, **malleable**, **ductile**, **transparent**, translucent, opaque, **conductor**, **insulator**, pottery, **ceramics**, plastics, metals, fibres, alloys, **raw materials**, **products**, physical change, chemical change, **solidification**, **condensation**, **melting** point, **freezing** point, **boiling** point, **evaporation**, **casting**, **atoms**, **soluble**, **insoluble**, **solute**, **solvent**, saturated, mixture, **element**, **distillation**, **desalination**, chemical reaction, **reactants**, products, **compounds**, word equation, heat, light, sound, **radiant energy**, **geothermal** energy, food energy, **kilojoules**, potential energy, kinetic energy, force, **inertia**, reaction force, gravity, friction, **lubrication**, **bearings**, smoothing, streamlining, machines, **pulleys**, gear wheels, hydraulic.

Key facts

- Everything is made of matter and all matter is made of tiny particles.
- The way that particles are arranged in different kinds of matter affects the properties of the matter or the way that the matter behaves.
- Matter can change and when it changes it will have different properties.
- When matter changes, the change can be a physical change or a chemical change.
- Physical changes are usually reversible and no new substances are formed. A change of state is an example of a physical change.
- Chemical changes are usually not reversible and new substances are formed. Burning is an example of a chemical change.
- Energy can exist in many different forms such as heat, light and sound.
- Energy can change from one form to another.
- Friction has advantages and disadvantages.
- Forces can be used in everyday life to make things move, to slow them down and to speed them up.
- Simple machines can do work and make life easier.

Assessment tasks

Assessment aims to gather information on how well students have achieved the outcomes of the strand **Science in the home**. A variety of strategies should be used: written, oral and practical.

Each assessment item should be based on criteria that have been clearly written down. Students should be told what the criteria are so that they know the basis for judgment of their achievement and demonstration of the outcomes.

Assessment should also be continuous and collected throughout the learning process by the completion of appropriate activities such as those indicated with the assessment icon in the 'For you to try' sections.

Major links to other subjects

Strand 3: Science in the home builds upon ideas introduced in Culture and Community at the elementary level and Environmental Studies at the lower primary level. At the upper primary level, **Science in the home** links to the strand Health of Individuals and Population in Personal Development. Aspects of different subjects can be integrated into activities such as:

- a project to improve life in the community
- collecting and analysing statistical data for specific groups in the community
- designing posters or performing a drama to relay the message of the benefits of using the methods of science

Links with other subjects are noted with an icon in the student books.

Teacher information

Learning about substances

In this topic students are introduced to the particle model of matter to explain the structure and behaviour of matter. The particle model is a theory and there is no easy way to demonstrate this to the students. If some students do not readily understand the idea then it is best not to spend too much time on the theory but move on to the more practical applications such as the properties of materials.

Properties of materials

The table on page 64 of the student book contains a list of words and meanings. Teachers should focus on developing the students' understanding of the meaning of different properties and the ways that we use materials rather than on remembering difficult new words.

Grouping solids

This way of grouping solids into five groups is only one possible method of classifying the solids that we use and is not meant to exclude others.

Metals and alloys

Metals and alloys are an important group so they are dealt with in greater detail than the other solids mentioned earlier. There are also links between this outcome and **8.4.1 Our Earth and its origin**, where students find out about the importance of the extraction of metals from rocks. These could be combined in a unit of work.

Changing matter

This topic is important because it introduces the concept of physical change and chemical change. Students should develop a clear understanding of each and be able to describe the difference and give practical examples.

Most teachers will not be able to demonstrate a wide range of chemical reactions since most schools do not have a specialist science laboratory with chemicals. However, teachers can still teach the basic concepts of a chemical change and demonstrate this with locally available resources. For example, every time we burn something or cook food then we are carrying out a chemical change.

Using energy in the home

The first three indicators in **7.3.3 Investigate how energy changes from one form to another** are covered under the heading 'Using heat, light and sound energy'.

Note that the last two indicators in 7.3.3 are also repeated in 7.3.5. They are:

- identify and make recommendations on how simple machines can make life easier through community field study

- construct a field survey or questionnaire which addresses the need for simple machines to do work.

These two indicators have been covered in **7.3.5 Identify and make recommendations on how simple machines can make life easier through community field study** since they form the core of this outcome. (*Upper Primary Syllabus*, pages 19 and 21)

Projects (page 104)
Students may need help in choosing and developing suitable projects. Teachers should make sure that all students are in a group and that the group has a clear purpose and time frame in which to work. All students should be actively involved and teachers will need to check regularly to make sure that each group is making progress.

The second project involves several steps: designing and administering the survey or questionnaire, analysing the results and making recommendations and possibly helping the community to implement one of them. Designing and carrying out a good survey and analysing the results uses a variety of important skills and students will need assistance in order to do it as well as they are able. Some examples of questions that can be used in a survey are given on pages 49–51.

Projects are a good opportunity for students to cooperate in groups over a period of time. It may help to link the outcome with an important event such as an end of term celebration or an open day. The students can then share what they have found out or produced with others.

Equipment needed for the activities and investigations

To complete the activities and investigations in this chapter each group of students will need the following.

For you to try (page 66)
- A variety of different everyday materials with different physical properties such as a plastic bag, glass, cup, saucepan, rubber, paper, copper wire, coins, steel nail, cotton, fish hook, fishing line, bilum, polystyrene, toothbrush etc.

For you to try (page 71)
- Local materials such as clay, stones and the seeds of plants. These should be as uniform in size and shape as you can find since they will be used to make particle models.

For you to try (page 72)
Investigation: The effect of heat when dissolving solutes
- A small glass jar, some salt, some sugar, cold water and hot water and a teaspoon.

For you to try (page 79)
Investigation: Leaving potato crisps in the air
- A packet of potato crisps or chips, a plate and a cover such as tea towel or piece of cloth.

For you to try (page 84)
Investigation: Feel the vibrations
- A radio and a balloon.

Investigation: Watch sound travel
- An old plastic bottle, a plastic bag, an elastic band, a candle and a pair of scissors.

Investigation: Changing sound
- Short pieces of bamboo, plastic tube or straws, a strip of flat timber or stiff card, rubber band or length of rubber inner tube.

Investigation: Bottle sounds
- Two identical glass bottles, some water and a spoon.

For you to try (page 88)
Investigation: Fruit drop
- A mug, a matchbox cover, a piece of card and a lemon or similar fruit.

Investigation: Five coin trick
- Five identical coins like 20t, 50t or K1 and a table knife.

For you to try (page 90)
Investigation: Turn the corner
- The lid from a cardboard carton and a small coin.

Investigation: Swing the bucket
- A bucket half full with water.

Investigation: Lift the ball
- A glass jar and a ball of plasticine about the size of a marble.

For you to try (page 93)
Investigation: How air pushes
- A bowl or bucket of water, a drinking glass or jam jar and a piece of paper.

Investigation: The force of air
- A large plastic shopping bag and a big book. The bag must not have any holes.

Investigation: Tug-of-war
- A piece of rope, bush vine or several laplaps tied together.

Investigation: Four against one
- Two strong, smooth sticks or broom handles, a long rope and some talcum powder

For you to try (page 98)
Investigation: Adding oil
- A smooth, flat surface like a glass louvre blade, a piece of flat iron or smooth, flat timber, a bottle top and some cooking oil or lubricating oil.

Investigation: Spinning around
- A drink can, fifteen marbles, some thin cardboard and sticky tape.

For you to try (page 100)
Investigation: Rice grain friction
- A small plastic bottle, uncooked rice and a knife.

Investigation: Putting on the brakes
- A matchbox, a matchstick, a needle and some thread.

For you to try (page 103)
- Students will need to be able to look at the engine of a car or truck to see the pulleys and fan belt. Note that in some modern cars the fan is not driven by the fan belt but is driven by an electric motor that turns on automatically when the engine gets hot. Care is needed when an engine is running because you may not see the fan turning. It is dangerous to put your hands inside the engine compartment when the engine is running. Loose clothes can also be dangerous because they can get caught and pull the person towards the engine.

Project (page 104)
- Students will need things with which to make instruments such as glass bottles and lengths of bamboo tube or plastic tube.

Answers and explanations

For you to try (page 63)

1 Answers will vary but some possible responses are shown below:

Matter that is used every day		
Solids	**Liquids**	**Gases**
clothes	kerosene	air
paper	cooking oil	oxygen
pencil	cordial	carbon dioxide
firewood	shampoo	
bilum	dishwashing liquid	
money	bleach	
fishing line	disinfectant	
glass	beer	
food	petrol	
tools	diesel **fuel**	
soil	engine oil	
road	two-stroke oil for outboard motors	
plate		
toothbrush		

2 **Investigation: Making a gas**
This experiment requires some skill to put the balloon quickly on the neck of the bottle. The second part of the experiment makes use of the fact that carbon dioxide is heavier than air and so it can be poured out of the bottle. Some skill is needed in order to hold the bottom of the bottle only slightly higher than the mouth so that the gas is poured out but the vinegar and bicarbonate of soda stay inside the bottle.

3
- The particles in a solid are held together very strongly and although the particles can move they cannot move past each other. These strong forces of attraction are the reason why a solid has a fixed size and shape.
- The particles in a liquid are held together by strong forces of attraction but not as strong as those in a solid. The particles are able to move easily past each other and so a liquid will always take up the shape of the container and can flow along pipes and tubes.
- The particles in a gas are well spaced and the forces between them are weak. Because the particles can move about quickly and easily the gas spreads out and fills the container. In other words a gas has no fixed size or shape.

For you to try (page 66)

1 The range of materials that students collect will vary and be able to be classified in several different ways depending on the properties that the students choose. Students should be encouraged to think about a range of properties and should realise that materials have a number of properties. For example, fishing line combines the properties of being light, strong, flexible and waterproof.

2 **a** A knife should be made of material that is strong and can be made sharp and will stay sharp. We may also want the knife to be flexible, like a grass knife. (An interesting comparison is disposable plastic knives that are used for parties and on aeroplanes.)

b The handle of a kettle should be a poor conductor of heat so that we do not burn our hands when we pick it up when it is hot. The shape and surface should provide a good grip so that we do not easily drop the kettle when our hands are wet.

c The bottom of a saucepan should be made of material that is a good conductor of heat so that the food can cook without using too much fuel. The material should be able to be made into different shapes and should not be too heavy. We should also be able to clean the saucepan easily.

d The covering of an electric wire should be a poor conductor of electricity. It should be able to be **moulded** around the wire and should be flexible and waterproof. It should be made of something that animals don't want to eat (rats sometimes chew wires) and should not be biodegradable.

e The window of a bathroom or toilet should be translucent or opaque. Light should be able to pass through the window but people should not be able to see inside.

3 Answers will vary but some possible metal objects are shown below:

Metals	Alloys
Aluminium saucepan	Steel bush knife—made from iron and carbon
Copper water pipe	**Brass** lock, brass tap—made from copper and zinc
Lead fishing sinker	**Stainless steel** spoon—made from iron, chromium, manganese, nickel
Lead battery	**Solder** on water tank—made from copper and tin
Corrugated iron roof (iron coated with zinc)	

For you to try (page 68)

1

Physical changes that are useful	Physical changes that are not useful
Chopping firewood	Tyres wearing out
Making sago	Clothes or a pair of thongs wearing out
Sugar dissolving in tea or coffee	A bridge being washed away after heavy rain
Sharpening a grass knife	The sand on a beach being carried away by a storm
New soil being left behind after a flood	Tearing somebody's clothes
Boiling water to make tea	Breaking a clay pot or a window
Freezing water to make ice blocks	Getting a puncture
Hanging out clothes to dry in the sunshine	A car crash that changes the shape of the bodywork of the car

For you to try (page 71)

1 The clay, stones, or the seeds of plants should be arranged in neat rows and layers to build geometric shapes (like cubes or pyramids) that represent different solids. For example, particles of sugar are shaped like a cube. Fruit and seeds as big as dry coconuts can be used for this activity.

3

Changing state			
Change of state	**Name of change**	**Change in energy**	**Change to particle movement**
Solid to liquid	Melting	Energy gained	Move more freely
Gas to liquid	Condensation	Energy added	Move less freely
Liquid to gas	Evaporation	Energy removed	Move more freely
Liquid to solid	Solidification or freezing	Energy added	Move less freely

For you to try (page 72)

1 **Investigation: The effect of heat when dissolving solutes**
Students should find that sugar or salt dissolves more easily in hot water than in cold water.

For you to try (page 74)

1 A physical change is one that occurs to matter when no new substances are formed. For example, when matter changes state a physical change occurs.
2 Energy has to be supplied to a substance or taken away before it changes state.
3 Examples will vary but might include sharpening a pencil, cutting firewood, cutting grass, clothes drying on a washing line, boiling water to make tea, adding sugar to a cup of tea, washing rice to get rid of insects and dirt etc.
4 **a** When wet clothes are hanging on a line the heat from the Sun makes the water evaporate leaving the clothes dry. The water in the clothes changes state from liquid to gas and no new substances are formed.
b When we scrape and squeeze coconut we break the meat of the coconut into lots of small pieces which allows the cream or oil to be squeezed out. No new substances are formed and so this is a physical change.
c When we put some sugar in hot water the sugar dissolves and although it cannot be seen it can still be tasted. This change is reversible and we can get the sugar back again by heating the water to make the water evaporate.
5 Each person needs one litre of fresh water per day.
There are four people in total so four litres per day are required.
If you are stuck for a week you need four litres per day multiplied by seven, or 28 litres in total.
A **solar still** requires 10 litres of sea water to produce one litre of fresh water.
So you need 10 multiplied by 28 or 280 litres of sea water to obtain enough fresh water.

For you to try (page 79)

1 **Investigation: Leaving potato crisps in the air**
Students should find that after a day or two the potato crisps become soft and are no longer crunchy so they will not make a noise when we eat them. Water is absorbed from the air and so they are no longer crisp. This is a physical change. However, because most chips are deep fried they contain oil which can also change when it is exposed to the air for too long. When oils or fats change in this way they are described as rancid.
2 A physical change is one in which no new substances are formed, energy change is not usually involved and it can often be reversed. A chemical change is where one or more new substances are formed, energy is given out or taken in and it is usually difficult to reverse.
3

	Type of change	
Example of change	**Physical**	**Chemical**
Coffee beans drying in the sun	✓	
Candle wax melting	✓	
Iron rusting		✓
Sharpening a bush knife	✓	
A match burning		✓
Meat being cooked		✓
Putting coffee into hot water	✓	
Grass cuttings decaying		✓
Peeling vegetables	✓	
Digesting food		✓
Cleaning a paintbrush with water	✓	

4 Answers will vary but useful chemical changes might include: cooking food, burning firewood, children and animals growing, people digesting food to get energy to do work, burning fuel in engines.

5 Answers will vary but chemical changes that are not useful might include the following:
- Food going rotten—which can make people sick or waste food.
- Burning food or something being destroyed by fire.
- A corrugated iron roof or water tank going rusty—so that it leaks and must be replaced.
- A bathroom floor or veranda becoming rotten and unsafe to walk on because it is always getting wet.
- People getting sick from chewing betel nut or smoking.

6 **a** In a raw egg the yolk is yellow and the white is clear and colourless. They are both liquid. After cooking the main change in appearance is the white, which really looks white. The yolk is still yellow but may have changed slightly. Both the yolk and white also change from a liquid to solid during cooking.

b Iron is a silver grey metal before it starts to rust. After rusting, the iron has a red coating which can begin to form in a few hours. After many years of rusting the iron can be eaten away.

c Magnesium is a silver grey metal that is usually in the form of a strip. When it burns, a white ash (magnesium oxide) is formed and a bright light is given out.

7 Students will come up with different ideas, but sensible choices would include:
- physical changes such as changes of state or making and separating mixtures
- chemical changes such as cooking and burning.

8 There are several ways for students to write acceptable, simple word equations and some examples are shown below:

a wood + air (oxygen) → ash + heat energy
b raw sweet potato + heat → cooked sweet potato
c raw meat + fat + heat → cooked meat
d fishing hook + water + air (oxygen) → rusty fish hook
e dry cell → casing + chemicals.

For you to try (page 84)

1 **Investigation: Feel the vibrations**
Students will feel few, if any, vibrations when the balloon is held away from the radio but when the balloon is closer to the radio they will feel vibrations. The vibrations will be felt more easily when the volume is turned up. The sound from the radio speaker makes the air vibrate and these vibrations make the air inside the balloon vibrate.

2 **Investigation: Watch sound travel**
The plastic bottle with a piece of plastic bag fixed over the bottom acts just like a drum. When students hit the end it will make a sound. The candle flame near the mouth of the bottle will also move at the same time because the sound makes the particles of air vibrate inside the bottle and this movement is passed on to the candle. The experiment shows that when we make a sound the air moves.

3 **Investigation: Changing sound**
This simple experiment will allow students to discover the relationship between the length of the tube and the pitch of the sound. The pitch of a sound tells us whether the sound is high or low. Bigger and longer tubes will make a lower sound.

4 **Investigation: Bottle sounds**
This simple experiment will allow students to discover the relationship between the amount of water or air in the bottle and the pitch of the sound. When we hit the bottles, the bottle with less water will make a sound with a higher pitch. When we blow into the bottles, the bottle with more air will give a sound with a lower pitch.

5 Answers will vary depending on the area, but some possible responses are shown below:

Name of instrument	How is the sound made?	Which part vibrates?
Kundu	Hitting the skin with the palm of the hand	The skin and the air inside the drum
Garamut or slit drum	Hitting the outside of the garamut with a stick	The wooden sides of the drum and the air inside
Pan pipes or conch shell	Blowing over the end of the tube or the hole	The air inside the pipe or shell
Bamboo band	Hitting the end of the tube with an old thong	The air inside the tube
Guitar or ukulele	Playing the strings with the hands or a plectrum	The string vibrates (the sound is increased by the sound box)
Rattle	Shaking in the hand	The seed cases from which the rattle is made

6 Answers will vary. Some ideas are shown in the table below:

Ways that energy can help people		
Example	**Energy change**	**Use or effect**
Heat—cooking food	From energy stored in fuel to heat energy	Allows people to eat food that must be cooked first
Heat—making copra	From energy stored in firewood to heat energy	Allows people to earn money from selling copra
Light—kerosene lamp	From energy stored in kerosene to heat energy	Allows people to see at night
Light—torch	From chemical energy in dry cell to electrical energy to light energy	Allows people to go fishing at night
Sound—garamut	From moving energy to sound energy	Allows people to send messages
Sound—radio	From chemical energy in dry cell to electrical energy to sound energy	Allows people to hear news and messages and listen to music

Ways that energy is not helpful or may be harmful		
Example	**Energy change**	**Effect**
Heat—burning the skin	From energy stored in fuel to heat energy	Person feels pain, skin can be damaged or person may die
Heat—burning a house or building	From energy stored in wood to heat energy	House or building destroyed by fire
Light—looking at a bright light e.g. the Sun	From energy in the Sun to light energy	The person may not be able to see for a while or may become blind
Light—car headlights from other cars	From chemical energy in a battery to electrical energy to light energy	Driver may not be able to see properly and may crash
Sound—very loud noise from machines	From moving energy to sound energy	May cause pain or deafness if it continues for a long time
Sound—very loud music late at night	From electrical energy to sound energy	People living nearby may not be able to sleep

For you to try (page 86)

1 Food is needed to provide energy for all the activities that we do such as walking, running, working, playing sport, thinking and breathing. Food is also needed to build and repair our bodies. People who need more food than normal are children who are growing, people who are sick and women who are pregnant.

For you to try (page 88)

1 **Investigation: Fruit drop**
When the card is pulled out the fruit will drop into the mug. This is because the fruit has inertia and is under the force of gravity. The fruit is not pulled sideways when the card is pulled out.

2 **Investigation: Five coin trick**
Only the bottom coin will move sideways when it is hit with a knife because the inertia of the coins means that they will continue to remain at rest unless a force is applied to them. No force is applied to the other coins.

For you to try (page 90)

1 **Investigation: Turn the corner**
When the lid is moved, a force is also applied to the coin and so it begins to move. When the lid is turned to one side, the coin will try to continue moving in the same direction. This is because of the inertia of the coin.

2 **Investigation: Swing the bucket**
The water will remain inside the bucket because the force of swinging the bucket round holds the water in place.

3 **Investigation: Lift the ball**
When the glass jar is lifted as it is still being rotated, the ball of plasticine will continue to move in a circle inside the jar and so will be lifted with the jar.

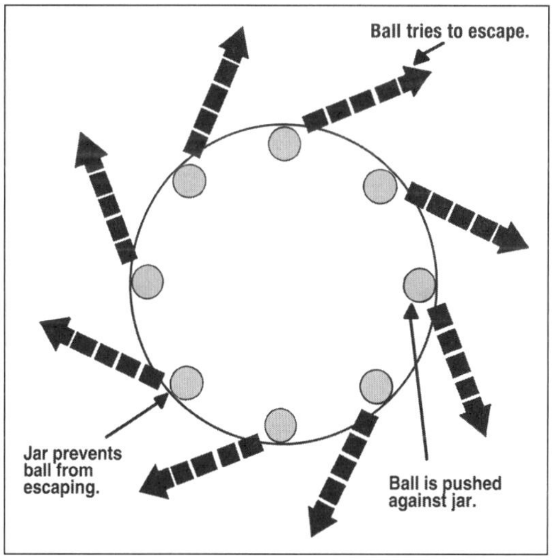

For you to try (page 93)

1 The force of gravity.
- Magnetic forces—like those in the door of a fridge, compasses, electric motors and generators, in radios and computers.
- Electrical forces—like those that make synthetic clothes stick to our bodies.
- Elastic forces—like those in a foam rubber mattress, a spring and a rubber.
- Friction—that allows things to move and to stop.

2
- The parachute is a simple and effective way to make something slow down when it is falling through the air. However, parachutes can also be used to slow things down when they are travelling along the ground. For example, parachutes can be used to slow down an aeroplane that has just landed, or to slow down a racing car that is travelling very fast. Boats on the open sea can also use a special parachute called a sea anchor to slow them down in a storm or when people are fishing. The parachute spreads out in the water and acts like brakes slowing the boat down and preventing it from moving too far.
- A larger parachute will make something slow down more quickly, but the material should be light and strong. Putting holes in the parachute will mean that the parachute is less effective at slowing down, but holes can be used to allow some of the air to escape so that the parachute does not tear.

3

- The brakes on a bicycle.
- Holding a paddle flat in the water to slow down a canoe.
- A parachute or sea anchor.
- Putting the engine of a boat in reverse so that the propeller turns the other way.
- Putting the jet engine of an aeroplane into reverse thrust when landing.

4

- Walking faster.
- Pedalling faster on a bicycle.
- Giving more fuel to an engine.

5 **Investigation: How air pushes**

The crumpled paper inside the drinking glass or jam jar will not get wet and the water will not go far inside the glass. This is because the air inside the glass is squashed by the water but pushes back against the water.

6 **Investigation: The force of air**

This surprising experiment shows the force of air. When the investigation is set up carefully with a suitable size plastic bag and big book, it is possible for one student to lift another just by blowing into the bag. The person blowing must hold the bag to make a mouthpiece to blow into and must hold it closed in between breaths so that the air does not escape. The bag must not have any holes.

7 **Investigation: Tug-of-war**

- When both sides pull equally then the forces are in opposite directions but the same size and the rope does not move.

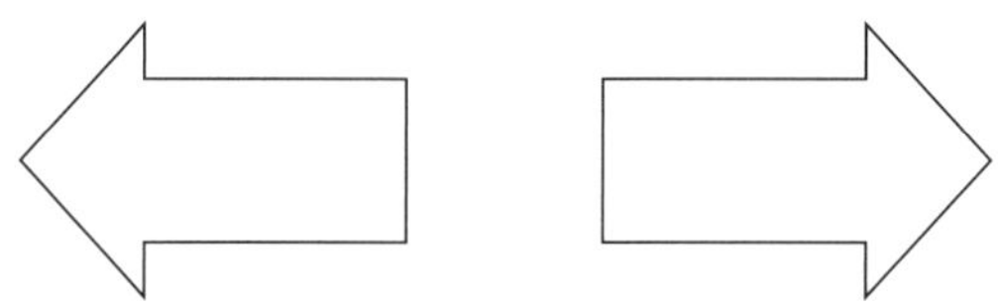

- When the side on the left pulls more than the side on the right the forces are in opposite directions but the force on the left is greater and the rope moves to the left.

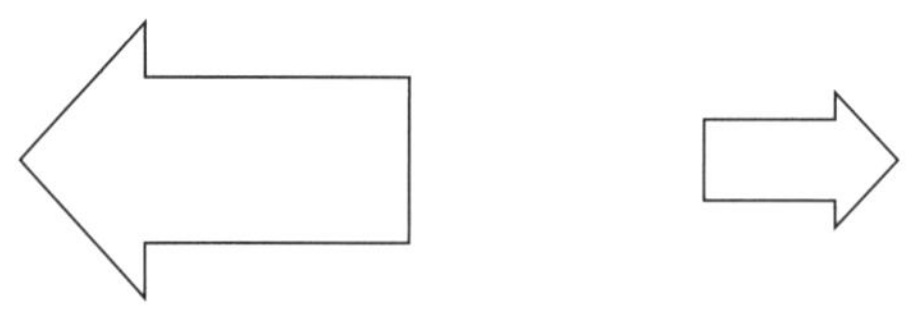

- When the side on the right pulls more than the side on the left the forces are in opposite directions but the force on the right is greater and the rope moves to the right.

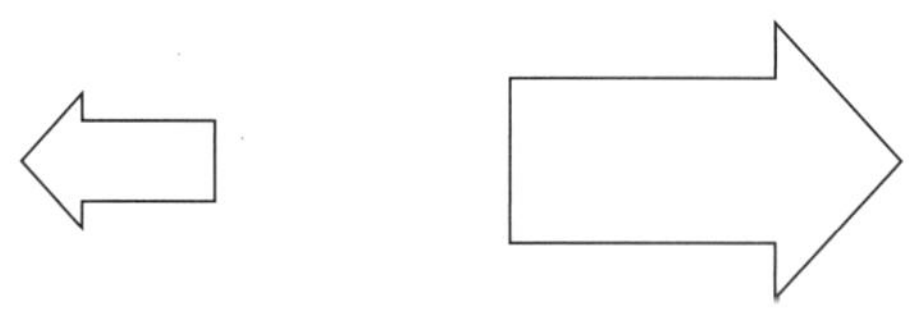

8 **Investigation: Four against one**

In this investigation one person can usually pull against four because each of the sticks is acting like a pulley wheel that reduces the size of the force that is needed (This gives a mechanical advantage, a topic that will be covered in Grade 8.)

For you to try (page 98)

1 **Investigation: Adding oil**

Adding oil to a smooth, flat surface like a glass louvre blade will reduce the friction even further and the bottle top will slide along more easily and travel further.

2 **Investigation: Spinning around**

When the can is standing on the collar it will turn, but not so easily, because of the friction between the collar and the table. When the marbles are placed underneath the collar the can will turn very easily because the marbles act like ball bearings and will turn as the can is turned. Only a small surface area of each marble is in contact with the table and with the next marble and so friction is very much reduced.

For you to try (page 100)

1 **Investigation: Rice grain friction**

In this unusual experiment the rice grains are packed so tightly in the bottle that the force between the rice grains and the knife is so strong that when the knife is lifted it will not come out of the rice but will lift up the whole bottle of rice too.

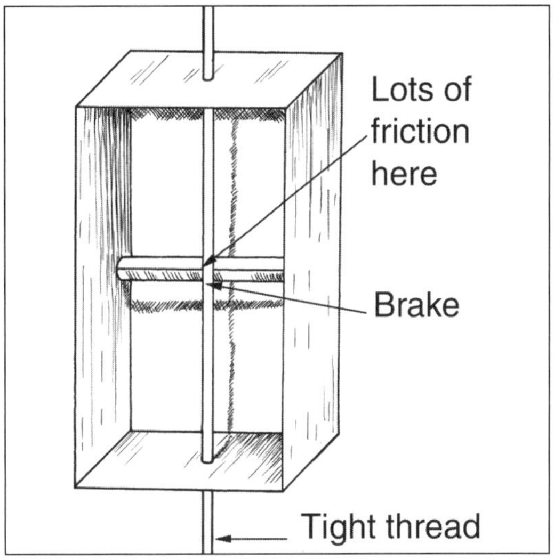

2 **Investigation: Putting on the brakes**

When the thread is held tight the matchbox lid will not fall because the thread will push against the matchstick and the friction acts like a brake. When the thread is loose it can easily move around the matchstick and so there is no friction and the matchbox lid will fall due to gravity.

3 The diagram or poster should be similar to one on page 96 of the student book.

4 For a cyclist riding a bicycle

a friction needs to be largest between the feet and the pedals, the hands and the handlebars, the tyres and the road and between the brakes and the rim of the wheel, and between the rider's bottom and the saddle.

b friction needs to be smallest in the bearings of the wheels, in the pedals, chain, **gears** and steering (the chain and gears both depend on friction but we still lubricate them so that they will work smoothly).

5 Oil is used to reduce friction in door hinges, nuts and bolts, engines, gearboxes, ball bearings and roller bearings.

6 If the engine of a car ran out of oil the moving parts like the pistons and bearings would overheat and expand and the engine would stop working. This is sometimes described as the engine seizing.

7 For each of the following, describe how friction is reduced:

a by adding oil to the **axle** so that the wheel can turn more easily

b the grease on the pole acts as a **lubricant** and there is very little friction between the pole and the arms and legs of the person trying to climb the pole

c the shape of a jet aeroplane is streamlined to reduce friction when it is flying at high speed and the painted metal surface is also smooth

d the hull of a canoe has a streamlined shape and is usually made smooth by rubbing with sandpaper

e when a boat rests on logs as it is pulled out of the water only the keel of the boat touches the logs and this reduces the area of the surfaces that are in contact with each other and so reduces the friction. The logs are acting like bearings and grease can also be used between the logs and the keel to reduce the friction further.

8

Diagram	Surfaces that the friction acts between	Friction used for
a	The person's fingers and the controls of the radio	Turning the radio on and off, tuning the radio, adjusting the volume
b	The person's hands and the rope	Pulling on the rope to lift the bucket
c	The person's hand and the handle of the grass knife	Holding the grass knife so that we can swing the grass knife and cut the grass
d	The bottom of the sports shoe (sole) and the ground	Moving forward quickly, changing directions, slowing down
e	The tread of the tyre and the road	Making the car move forward, changing direction by going round corners and slowing down
f	The hand of a person and the handle of the screwdriver	Tightening screws, undoing screws, removing the lid from a tin of paint
g	The metal grater and the meat of the dry coconut	Grating coconut into small pieces so that we can get the oil and flavour out of the coconut
h	The teeth of the saw and the wood	Cutting large pieces of wood into smaller pieces with a special shape
i	The head of the match and the special rough strip on the side of the box	Making the head of the match hot so that it begins to burn
j	The belt and the pulley wheels of the machine	Making machines e.g. cassette recorders

9 Answers will vary but the main ideas are outlined below:

- Friction has both advantages and disadvantages. Friction is needed to make things move and without friction nothing would be able to move. Friction between our feet and the ground allows us to walk and to run, to change direction and to slow down. Friction allows us to pick things up with our hands and to scratch ourselves when we feel itchy. When we hold tools like an axe to cut firewood then we are making use of friction. Friction also allows us to make a fire. Traditional methods of starting a fire and matches both depend on the heat that comes from rubbing two things together. Friction is important in machines too. We can ride a bicycle because of the friction between our feet and the pedals and between the tyres and the road. And we make the bicycle stop because of friction between the brakes and the rim of the wheel. All engines depend on friction to be able to work.
- Friction can also be a problem for the same reasons that it is useful. For example, the heat that comes from friction can make a machine get too hot and catch fire. The moving parts will expand and the machine will stop working. This is why machines have ways to carry away the heat caused by friction. For example, engines use lubrication, moving water and moving air to cool them. Friction also makes parts wear out. For example, the brake blocks on a bicycle and the brake pads on a car will both wear out from time to time and need replacing. We cannot use lubrication to stop them wearing out because then the brakes would not work. However, we can use oil and grease to lubricate the moving parts in an engine, gearbox, and bearings to reduce the friction so that they do not wear out so quickly.

For you to try (page 102)

1 Simple machines like scissors and pliers are called double **levers** because they are made from two levers that are joined together through a pivot that acts as the fulcrum for both levers.

2 The propeller of a boat is usually made of two or more curved blades that are joined together at the centre. The propeller fits on to the shaft so that it can turn like a fan. As the propeller turns, the curved

surface of each blade pushes against the water and makes the boat move forward. It is also called a screw because it works in a similar way to a screw in a piece of wood.

3 As you turn the handle of a car jack the threaded shaft in the centre pulls the two ends closer together. This has the effect of opening the arms of the jack like opening a pair scissors and so the car is lifted.

4 A vice is made from two jaws that hold things that are being made or repaired. One jaw is fixed and does not move. The other jaw can move. There is a handle outside the moveable jaw and this handle is connected to a screw. There is also a nut inside the moveable jaw. As you turn the handle clockwise the screw turns inside the nut which makes the jaw move to grip whatever is between the jaws. As you turn the handle counter-clockwise the screw turns inside the nut which makes the jaw move back, releasing the grip.

For you to try (page 103)

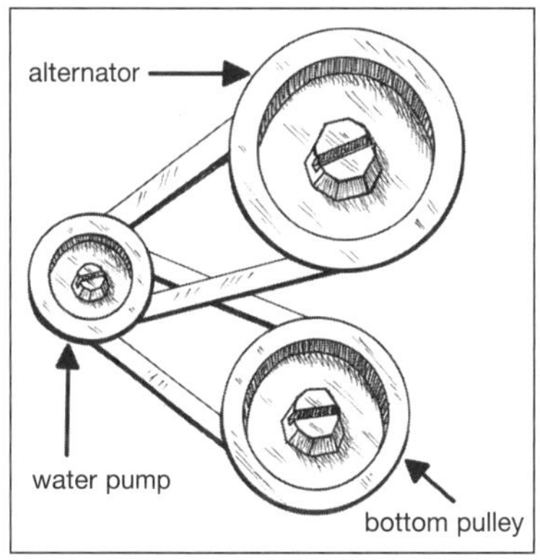

1 If the fan belt breaks or comes off then the alternator will not work so the battery will not be charged and will go flat. Also the water pump will not turn so water will not move around the engine. The water in the top of the radiator may boil, the engine will get too hot and may seize or stop working.

2 If the two students are riding different bicycles then the one that is pedalling faster must have a smaller crank or main gear wheel. The smaller gear wheel has to be turned more times in order to travel at the same speed as the other student.

If the students are riding identical bicycles then they must be using different gears. The student who is pedalling faster must be using a lower gear (which is smaller) and has to turn more times to travel at the same speed as the other student.

3 The most important properties of the rubber timing belt of a car or truck engine are that it must be strong and flexible and must not stretch or break. The timing belt is a very important part of the engine and it will not work without it. The timing belt opens and closes the valves that allow fuel into the engine and exhaust gases out of the engine. If the timing belt slips or breaks then the engine will not only stop working but it will be damaged.

Project (page 104)

1 Students will need to experiment with different size bottles and with different amounts of water. There are eight musical notes in an octave and so with eight bottles students should be able to play some simple tunes. They will need to use their own judgment and knowledge of popular music and church music to put different amounts of water in a set of bottles until it sounds right. Different sets of bottles could be played together by a number of students to make the sound bigger and more interesting as the sounds combine together.

2 The questions in a survey must be written with the objectives of the survey and the characteristics of the community clearly in mind.

Questions that are used in a survey or questionnaire are generally of two types:

- **Open-ended** questions that give the person much freedom in the way that they answer the question. These questions are usually easier to write but harder to analyse because the wide range of responses can make it difficult to collate the information and make generalisations. When we interview a person we usually use open-ended questions.

- **Multiple-choice** or **fixed-response** questions that have more structure and guide the person to answer in particular ways by ticking various boxes. These are harder to write but it is easier to analyse the responses because you can get numbers and percentages of people who respond in a particular way and can then make generalisations that can lead to recommendations.

Examples of multiple-choice or fixed-response questions:

Q Which of the following simple machines do you use at your home? (You can tick more than one box.)

Steps or a ladder to get inside the house	
Scissors	
A screwdriver	
Anything with wheels and an axle like a trolley or push cart	
A ramp—for example, to walk up to the house	
Anything with a pulley—for example, a bucket shower	
Anything with gear wheels like a rotary clothes line or Hills hoist	
Other—please specify	

Q Which of the following simple machines do you use **outside** your home—in the garden or at work? (You can tick more than one box.)

Digging stick	
Crowbar—for example, for moving rocks or logs	
Pinch bar—for example, for opening wooden packing cases	
Anything with wheels and an axle like a trolley or push cart	
A ramp—for example, to load 200-litre drums of fuel on a truck or boat	
Anything with a pulley—for example, on a sailing canoe or boat	
Anything with gear wheels like a bicycle, car or truck	
Other—please specify	

Examples of open-ended questions:

Q Thinking about the work that you need to do inside your home, are there any simple machines that you do not have but would help you?

Q Thinking about the work that you need to do outside your home, are there any simple machines that you do not have but would help you or the community?

Many surveys combine both types of questions, often with multiple-choice questions first and then some open-ended questions at the end.

Keep the survey as short as possible. Do not ask questions if you are not going to use the information. For example, if you are interested in the work done by men and women and by people of different ages then you need to record their sex and age, but if you are not interested in these differences then it is a waste of time asking their age and recording their sex.

Students and teachers will also need to think about the following:

- How will you obtain permission and agreement from people to take part in the survey?

- How many people will take part in the survey?
- How will the survey be given—will the person fill in their own survey or will the student ask the question and then fill it in for them?
- What will you do if the person does not understand the question?
- When will the survey take place?
- How will you collate the results and make general conclusions?

Summary questions

1 A
2 D
3 D
4 A
5 B
6 B
7 A
8

Radiant energy	Use or effect	Answer
A Heat	**1** Taking photographs to see inside the body or inside suitcases at airports	**G**
B Light	**2** Cooking and heating	**A**
C Radio waves	**3** Cooking and communication	**D**
D Microwaves	**4** Radio communication	**C**
E Infra-red rays	**5** Causes sunburn of the skin	**F**
F Ultra-violet rays	**6** Heating	**E**
G X-rays	**7** Allows animals to see	**B**

9 C
10

	Statement	T or F?
A	Friction is always a problem and should be reduced.	F
B	New tyres give a better grip than old tyres.	T
C	Making surfaces smooth increases friction between them.	F
D	Increasing the force between two surfaces increases the friction.	T
E	Oil and grease are lubricants that increase friction.	F
F	Making the bottom of a canoe smooth helps it move more easily through the water.	T
G	Ball bearings help wheels to turn more easily.	T
H	A file used to sharpen a bush knife will work better if we put oil or grease on it.	F

11 B
12 Everything is made of matter and all matter is made of tiny **particles.** The way that particles are arranged in different kinds of matter affects the **properties** of the matter or the way that the matter behaves. Matter can change and when it changes it will have different properties. When matter changes, the change can be a physical change or a chemical change. Physical changes are usually **reversible** and no new substances are formed. A change of **state** is an example of a physical change. Chemical changes are usually not reversible and new **substances** are formed. Burning is an example of a chemical change.

Energy can exist in many different forms such as heat, light and sound. Energy can change from one **form** to another. **Forces** can be used in everyday life to make things move, to slow them down and to speed them up. The force of **friction** is needed to allow things to move and friction also slows things down, so friction has advantages and disadvantages. Simple machines can do **work** and make life easier.

STRAND 4 Earth and beyond

About this strand

This strand builds on the ideas in basic **geology** and **astronomy** that were introduced in Grade 6. It consists of two sub-strands. The first sub-strand **Our Earth and its origin** begins by reviewing the formation of different kinds of rocks, **weathering** and **erosion**, and the **rock cycle**. **Sedimentary rocks** are covered in more detail and this leads into a description of the formation of various kinds of **fossils**. The sub-strand concludes by looking at the uses of fossils and the way in which they can help us to understand a little about the plants and animals that lived in the past, and the age of sedimentary rocks in which fossils are found.

In the second sub-strand, **Space exploration**, students find out about the **solar system** and the various bodies that are found in space such as **comets**, **meteors**, the **asteroid** belt and **planets**. The strand develops by looking at the movement of various heavenly bodies and the effect of these movements. First, the rotation of the Earth on its **axis** and the way in which this causes day and night. Second, the orbit of the Earth around the Sun and the way in which this causes the seasons. Third, the orbit of the Moon around the Earth and the way in which this causes the **phases of the Moon** and the **tides**. The strand concludes by looking at the ways in which **solar** and **lunar eclipses** occur.

Sub-strands 1 and 2

Main ideas

Sub-strand 1: Rocks can be formed in different ways and the materials that make up rock can move in a cycle. Sedimentary rocks are formed from the **sediments** that are carried by rivers and then deposited. When plants and animals die they can become buried with the sediments and form fossils. Fossils can be used to work out how long ago a sedimentary rock was formed and what plants and animals were living at that time.

Sub-strand 2: The solar system is made up of the Sun, planets, asteroids, meteors and comets. The rotation of the Earth on its axis and the orbit of the Earth around the Sun and the orbit of the Moon around the Earth cause things that affect our lives such as day and night, the seasons, tides and eclipses.

Key words

Igneous, sedimentary, metamorphic, weathering, erosion, fossils, **mineralisation**, moulds, casts, impressions, index, **universe**, **galaxy**, solar system, comet, meteor, asteroid, planet, **satellite**, season, axis, rotation, orbit, phase, tide, eclipse, solar, lunar.

Key facts

- Rock can be formed in different ways. For example, rock can be formed from volcanoes and from the sediments that are carried in water and settle on the bottom of the sea, lakes and swamps.
- The materials that make up rock can move in a cycle. Rock can be slowly weathered or worn away by ice, water and wind and the small particles can be carried or eroded by water and settle down as sediments. Over thousands of years the sediment can form layers of sedimentary rock.
- When plants and animals die they can become buried with the sediments and form fossils.
- Fossils are the preserved remains or traces of plants and animals that lived millions of years ago.
- Fossils can be used to work out how long ago a rock was formed and what plants and animals were living at that time.
- Our solar system consists of eight planets, together with their moons, the asteroids, meteors and comets.
- We can observe changes in the position of the planets, the Moon and the Sun and how these changes affect our way of life.
- The tilt of the Earth towards the Sun and the movement of the Earth around the Sun affect the length of day and night and the change of the seasons.
- The position of the Earth, Moon and Sun causes tides and eclipses.

Assessment tasks

Assessment aims to gather information on how well students have achieved the outcomes of the strand. A variety of strategies should be used: written, oral and practical.

Each assessment item should be based on criteria that have been clearly written down. Students should be told what the criteria are so that they know the basis for judgment of their achievement and demonstration of the outcomes.

Assessment should also be continuous and collected throughout the learning process by the completion of appropriate activities such as those indicated with the assessment icon in the 'For you to try' sections.

Major links to other subjects

Strand 4: Earth and beyond builds upon ideas introduced in Culture and Community at the elementary level and Environmental Studies at the lower primary level. At the upper primary level, **Earth and beyond** links to the strand Our culture, lifestyle and values in Personal Development. Aspects of different subjects can be integrated into activities such as:

- a project to improve life in the community
- collecting and analysing statistical data for specific groups in the community
- designing posters or performing a drama to relay the message of the benefits of using the methods of science.

Links with other subjects are noted with an icon in the student books.

Teacher information

The formation of rocks

The explanation of the formation of different rocks should remind students of what they learned in Grade 6 and of basic ideas such as weathering, erosion and the rock cycle. However, this information is really provided for the sake of completion and as a background since the main purpose is to describe the formation of sedimentary rocks in more detail. This leads to the way in which fossils are formed in rocks since this process can happen only in sedimentary rocks.

How fossils are formed

The three main methods in which fossils form in sedimentary rocks are described. These processes are complicated and explanations have been kept as simple as possible but provide enough information to make the difference clear. Students should not be expected to remember the details of how fossils form.

Other kinds of fossils

Although most fossils are found in rocks, they can also be found in **amber** which is the gum from a pine tree, in **coal** and in ice. Otzi the iceman is one of the most interesting discoveries ever to be made and scientists have found out a lot about the way that he lived.

Otzi the iceman

Otzi the iceman was found by two German tourists on 19 September 1991 in mountains known as the Alps on the border between Austria and Italy. The body was in an unusual position, lying face down with the left arm across the chest frozen in ice. It is not unusual for people to die in high mountains because of the cold weather and sudden storms and at first people thought that it was the body of a modern person.

Scientists examined the body, measured it and took X-rays as well as doing other investigations for several years. They found out that Otzi lived about 3300 BC or 5300 years ago and so he is the oldest and best-preserved fossil of this kind. When he died Otzi was about 165 cm tall, weighed about 38 kg and was about 46 years old. His body was covered in ice shortly after he died and remained covered in ice which helped to preserve it.

By looking at the contents of his **intestines**, scientists have worked out that he ate two meals not long before he died. One contained chamois meat, and the other red deer meat. Both these animals are found in the Alps. He had also eaten some grain, possibly in the form of bread, and some roots and fruits. There were also a lot of copper particles in his hair and scientists think that he may have been involved in smelting copper and making copper tools.

Other investigations have been carried out on the remains of his clothes and the many useful things he was carrying with him. He wore a cloak made from woven grass and a vest, a belt, a pair of leggings, a loincloth and shoes all made from leather. He also wore a bearskin cap with a leather chin strap. The shoes were waterproof and wide, and seemed to be designed for walking across the snow. The soles were made from bearskin, the upper part was made from deer skin and the netting from the bark of a tree. Soft grass was packed around the foot inside the shoe to act like warm socks. The vest, belt, leggings, and loincloth were made of vertical strips of leather sewn together with ligaments from muscles. His belt had a pouch sewn to it that contained a number of useful items: a scraper, drill, a bone awl for making holes and equipment for making fire.

The other tools that he was carrying included an axe made from copper with a wooden handle, a flint knife with a wooden handle and fourteen arrows with bone tips, wooden shafts and flint heads (two arrows were finished, twelve were not). He had a wooden bow about a metre long, although this was also not finished, two baskets and some berries.

He was also carrying two special mushrooms with leather strings through them. One of these is known to have antibacterial properties and scientists think that it was used as a medicine. The other was a type of dried fungus to be used as tinder to start a fire. A range of different equipment that he carried was used for starting a fire. These included pieces of over a dozen different plants as well as a piece of stone called flint and a stone called pyrite that can be used to make a spark.

Scientists have also tried to work out how Otzi died. He had what appears to be an arrowhead in his shoulder but the arrow shaft had been removed. He also had a deep wound on his thumb that went down to the bone and other cuts and bruises on his hands, wrists and chest. Traces of blood from four other people were also found on his clothes and his knife and an arrowhead. He may have been part of a group that was involved in a tribal fight. Scientists think that he may have died very quickly due to blood loss when the arrow cut an artery. However, it is also possible that after the arrow hit him he fell and hit his head on a rock or that he was hit on the back of the head by his attacker.

Scientists also think that he was part of a community that worked together. For example, the copper axe that he carried could not have been made by him alone. It would have required a group effort to mine, smelt and cast the copper axe head. This may show that the group was able to plan, prepare and cooperate in order to achieve its goals.

Fossil fuels

This topic also links with **7.3.3 Using energy in the home** in which students investigate how energy changes from one form to another.

Using fossils

Index fossils are also known as guide fossils or zone fossils. They are fossils that are used to define and identify geological time periods. They make use of the idea that, although different sediments may look different depending on the conditions in which they were laid down, they may include the same species of fossil.

If the fossil lived for a relatively short time (in geological terms, this means a few hundred thousand years), then it is certain that the sediments in which the fossil is found were deposited within that narrow time period. The shorter the lifespan of a fossil, the more precisely different sediments can be matched, and so fossils that evolved rapidly are particularly useful. The best index fossils are common, easy to identify, and have a broad distribution—otherwise the likelihood of finding and recognising one in the two sediments is low.

Ammonites are the best-known index fossils because they have these characteristics. Other important groups that provide index fossils are the corals and sea urchins. Fossils such as the teeth of mammals have also been used.

Geologists use both large fossils and microscopic fossils as index fossils. Large fossils are easy to see but are less common. Microscopic fossils are used by geologists looking for oil when they want accurate knowledge about the age of rocks.

The planets

Pluto was discovered in 1930 and was considered as the ninth planet of the solar system until 2006. However, in the late 20th and early 21st centuries, many objects similar to Pluto were discovered in the outer solar system. One of these was a body called Eris which is 27 percent more massive than Pluto. On 24 August 2006 a group of scientists known as the International Astronomical Union (IAU) defined the term 'planet' for the first time. This definition excluded Pluto from the group of planets, and reclassified it under the new category of **dwarf planet** along with Eris and Ceres. After the reclassification, Pluto was added to the list of minor planets and given the number 134340.

This is an example of the way in which scientists are able to change the way that they think when new evidence does not fit with previous ideas. Older science books will continue to show Pluto as a planet, but in this book it is described as a dwarf planet consistent with the new classification.

Teachers may like to discuss this change of classification with students, especially from the point of view of being confident about what we know and being willing to be proved wrong and willing to change our thinking.

Night and day

Because the Earth spins or rotates once every twenty-four hours countries close to the equator, like Papua New Guinea, usually have twelve hours of daylight and twelve hours of darkness. However, there are differences within Papua New Guinea. For example, because Manus Island is so close to the equator the length of the day and night will be almost the same all through the year. Further south, in Central Province and Milne Bay people will notice that the days are shorter in the middle of the year. For example, people can find that it is harder to get up in the morning and it is harder to do things outside in the late afternoon because it gets dark earlier.

People who live in temperate climates much further away from the equator experience even greater differences in the length of day and night.

Seasons

The table below is a more complete version of the one in the student book. Students should understand what causes seasons, especially in Papua New Guinea, but do not need to remember the details from other countries.

Solstice

A solstice occurs twice a year, whenever the Earth's axis tilts the most towards or away from the Sun, which causes the Sun to be farthest north or south at noon. At the solstice the Sun seems to stand still—its movement north or south is smallest. The term solstice can also be used in a wider sense as the date (day) that such a passage happens. The solstices, together with the equinoxes, are related to the seasons and in some cultures they are considered to start or separate the seasons. The table below summarises the solstices in both hemispheres.

Months	Countries	Season	Temperature	Length of day and night
December, January, February	Australia and New Zealand (southern hemisphere)	Summer	Warm or hot	Long days and short nights
	Europe, USA, Canada (northern hemisphere)	Winter	Cold—frost, snow and ice in some places	Short days and long nights
March, April, May	Australia and New Zealand (southern hemisphere)	Autumn	Getting cooler	Days getting shorter, nights getting longer
	Europe, USA, Canada (northern hemisphere)	Spring	Getting warmer	Days getting longer, nights getting shorter
June, July, August	Australia and New Zealand (southern hemisphere)	Winter	Cold—frost, snow and ice in some places	Short days and long nights
	Europe, USA, Canada (northern hemisphere)	Summer	Warm or hot	Long days and short nights
September, October, November	Australia and New Zealand (southern hemisphere)	Spring	Getting warmer	Days getting longer, nights getting shorter
	Europe, USA, Canada (northern hemisphere)	Autumn or fall	Getting cooler	Days getting shorter, nights getting longer

Date	Solstice	Length of day and night
June 20 or 21	Summer solstice in the northern hemisphere	Longest day and shortest night
	Winter solstice in the southern hemisphere	Shortest day and longest night
December 21 or 22	Winter solstice in the northern hemisphere	Shortest day and longest night
	Summer solstice in the southern hemisphere	Longest day and shortest night

Another interesting fact is that the earliest sunrise and latest sunset do not occur on the longest day. Similarly, the latest sunrise and earliest sunset do not occur on the shortest day. These times can vary by several weeks either side of the solstice and is due to the complicated orbit of the Earth around the Sun.

Equinox

An equinox occurs twice a year when the Sun can be observed to be directly above the equator. The equinoxes are the two days each year when the centre of the Sun spends an equal amount of time above and below the horizon at every place on Earth. Day and night are nearly the same length at the equinox but because of the way that light reaches the Earth from the Sun, the day is slightly longer—we still receive light from the Sun even after it has set below the horizon. The table below summarises the equinoxes in both hemispheres.

Date	Equinox	Length of day and night
March 20 or 21	Spring equinox in the northern hemisphere	Nearly the same
	Autumn equinox in the southern hemisphere	Nearly the same
September 22 or 23	Autumn equinox in the northern hemisphere	Nearly the same
	Spring equinox in the southern hemisphere	Nearly the same

Supplementary activities (for answers, see *Answers and explanations* section)

a Draw a table with two columns to describe some of the uses of different kinds of rock.
b Give some examples of different kinds of rocks and the ways in which we can tell how they formed.
c Briefly describe how fossils can form in rocks.
d What are fossil fuels? Why are they so important?
e Explain how fossils can be used to work out the age of a sedimentary rock.
f Why are fossils not found in igneous rock and only occasionally in metamorphic rock?
g How does the rotation of the Earth on its axis affect people and other living things?
h How does the orbit of the Earth around the Sun affect people and other living things?

Equipment needed for the activities and investigations

To complete the investigations and activities in this chapter each group of students will need the following.

For you to try (page 116)
Investigation: Weathering

- A small piece of sandstone rock, a piece of fencing wire, an empty tin, a funnel made from a plastic bottle, a piece of newspaper, and a magnifying glass.

For you to try (page 119)

Investigation: Collecting sediments

- The tube from the inside of a toilet roll, a piece of newspaper and different types of mud, fine soil or sediment each with a different colour in a tin (at least three different types).

Investigation: Making sedimentary rocks with fossils

- Some sand, gravel, soil with sticks and leaves removed or very fine silt, crushed lime, plaster of Paris, seashells or pieces of shell, small fish bones, old Tetrapak drink containers (250 mL), old tins or jars (for mixing plaster), and fine sandpaper.
- If you cannot obtain plaster of Paris, but can obtain a small amount of cement then you could use a very weak mix of sand and cement (called mortar) to hold the sedimentary rock together: use eight parts of sand to one part of cement. Mix the sand and water well first, then add enough water to make a thick mixture. Do not add too much water because it will take longer for the sedimentary rock to set. Then add the sediments and types of fossils as described in the table on page 120 of the student book.

For you to try (page 126)

Investigation: Making a model solar system

- A large sheet of paper and a selection of the common objects such as pins (with heads), pins with coloured plastic balls at the end, rice grains, seeds, marbles, polystyrene balls, lemon, ball made from woven pandanus, or similar objects and some glue.

Investigation: How far apart are the planets?

- Nine pieces of paper, a marker pen or crayon, and access to a space outside the classroom.

For you to try (page 129)

Investigation: Night and day

- A torch and a large ball or balloon as a model of the Earth (globe).

Investigation: One year and the seasons

- A pressure lamp or electric lamp and a large ball or balloon as a model of the Earth (globe).

For you to try (page 132)

Investigation: The phases of the Moon

- A pressure lamp or electric lamp and a large ball or balloon as a model of the Moon.

Projects (page 134)

1. **Make a fossil collection**
   - Samples of rock containing fossils from your area and other areas.
   - A box or tray in which to display the fossils.
   - Paper or card to make labels for the fossils.
2. **Make a sundial**
   - Some cardboard, glue, scissors and a copy of the **sundial** template (page 59).
   - An alternative is to make a human sundial (page 60). Lay out the hour marks using flat stones or concrete, and then let the user stand in a square marked with the month. The month squares are arranged to correct the sundial for the time of year. The user's head then forms the **gnomon** of the dial. If the sundial is made with stones or concrete blocks, it cannot be changed or destroyed, is fun to use and reasonably accurate.

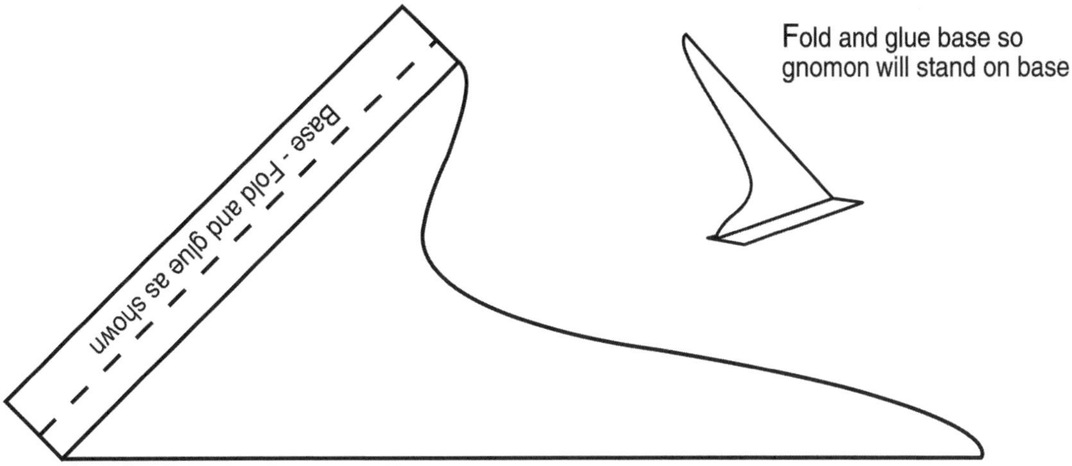
Base - Fold and glue as shown
Fold and glue base so
gnomon will stand on base

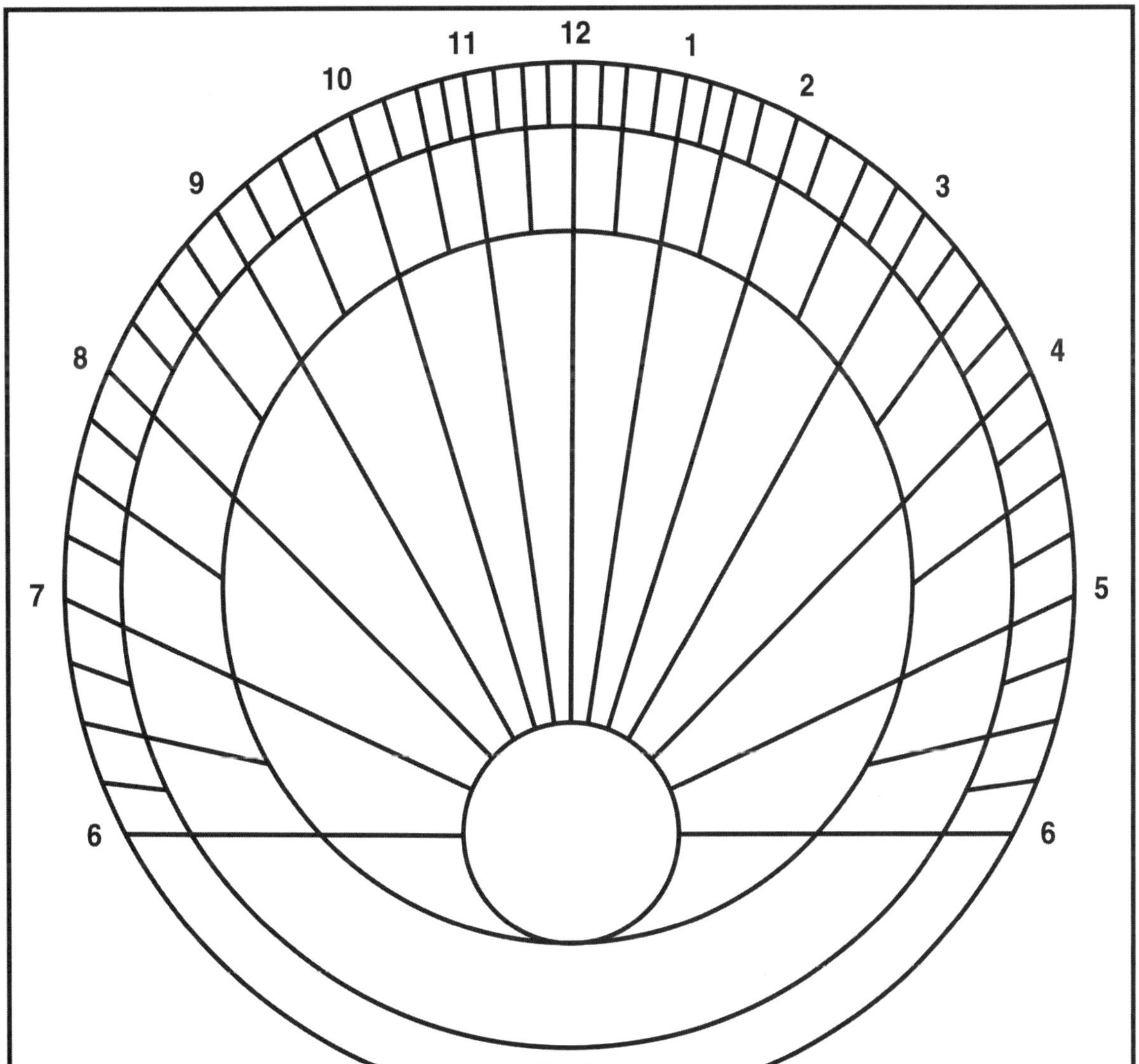
12
11
1
10
2
9
3
8
4
7
5
6
6
South

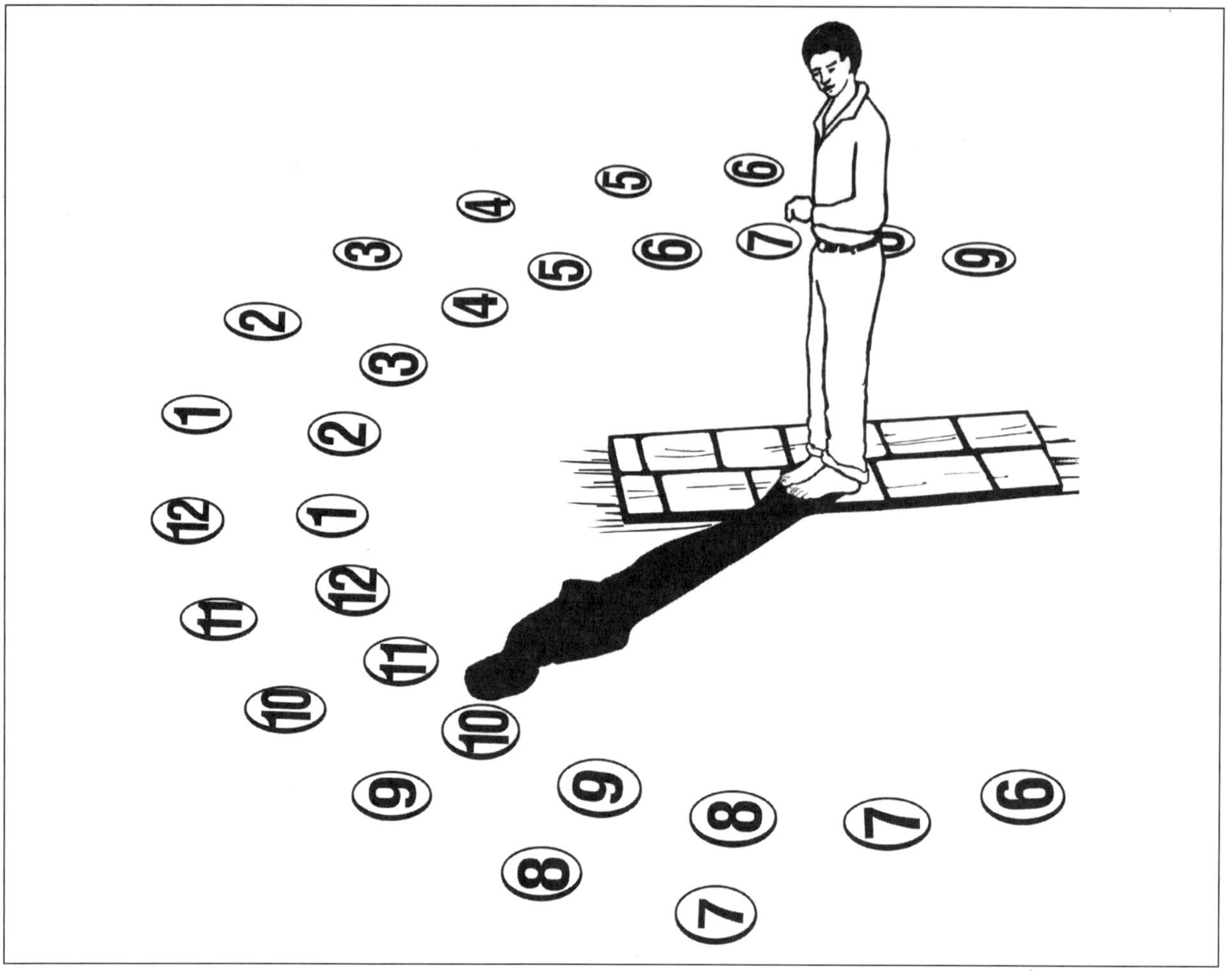

Answers and explanations

For you to try (page 116)

1 **Investigation: Weathering**

Students should see that the appearance of the rock begins to change. The outside will start to become rough and little pieces of rock that break off will be found on the filter paper. The purpose of rapid heating in a flame and cooling in water demonstrates the effect of weathering in nature, but speeds it up so that it can be seen more easily.

Supplementary activities

a Answers will vary, but some examples are given below:

Type of rock	Uses	Type of rock	Uses
River stones	Building walls and houses, mumus	Basalt	Making roads
Stone axe or adze	Cutting trees, making canoes	Granite	Building and making monuments
Obsidian	Spears, scrapers and sharp tools	Slate	Roof and floor tiles, paving, pool tables
Pumice	Making things smooth and cleaning skin	Marble	Floors and bathrooms

Earth and beyond

b Igneous rocks that are found in volcanic areas are usually very hard. This is because they were once molten magma deep inside the Earth that has come to the surface and cooled down. For example, obsidian is so hard that it looks like black glass. Some igneous rocks are full of holes that formed from bubbles of gases when the rock was still molten. Pumice is like this and is so light that it can float on water.

Sedimentary rocks, like sandstone and limestone, were made from layers of sediments that built up over thousands of years. We can sometimes see the layers and it is not so hard so we can cut it and use it for building.

Metamorphic rock, like slate and marble, is made from sedimentary rock and igneous rock that has been changed deep inside the Earth. We can see the layers in slate and this means that the rock can be split and cut more easily. This is how we are able to make slate tiles for floors and roofs. Because big sheets of slate are flat, we can also use it to make pool tables. Marble is another metamorphic rock that can be used to make floors and is also used in kitchens and bathrooms.

For you to try (page 119)

1 Investigation: Collecting sediments

The purpose of this investigation is to demonstrate the way in which sediments are formed in different layers. The result will be most convincing when mud or soil with different colours is used.

2 Investigation: Making sedimentary rocks with fossils

- The purpose of this investigation is to demonstrate the formation of different kinds of sedimentary rock. Students can choose to make conglomerate rock, sandstone, shale or limestone.
- Some conglomerate rock looks very much like concrete because of all the stones that are cemented together.

Supplementary activities

c Fossils can form in three main ways:

- When an animal dies in the sea it falls to the bottom and can be buried by sediments. The soft parts of the animal rot but the hard parts, like bones and teeth, do not rot. Over many years, more and more sediment covers the remains of the animal. The chemicals that make up the buried animal slowly change and the original minerals are replaced with minerals from the water and sediment. This makes a copy of the original animal that looks like rock.
- Sometimes an animal can be buried or trapped in mud, clay, or ash from a volcano which later harden around it. When the body decays it leaves a mould that shows the shape of the original animal. When the space is filled with another material such as sediment then it makes a cast of the original animal.
- An animal or plant can leave behind an impression in soft mud or sediment; for example, the leaves of a plant, footprints or the track of an animal. If the sediment or mud hardens into rock then a fossil is formed.

d Fossil fuels such as coal, oil and natural gas are the remains of plants and animals that lived a long time ago. They are important because they can be burned to give energy and are also used to make many other things. They are the most important source of energy used in the world today. However, because they are a non-renewable resource, some people are worried about what will happen when they run out.

Using fossils

Supplementary activities

e Fossils that lived for only a relatively short period of time can be used to work out the age of a sedimentary rock. If that fossil is found in a sedimentary rock then we can be confident that the animal lived and died at the same time as the sediments were forming on the bottom of the sea. So if we know when that animal was alive then we can work out the age of the rock in which the fossil was found. This method will only work for some fossils.

f Fossils are not found in igneous rock because these rocks form from hot, molten rock that comes from deep in the Earth. Plants and animals do not live deep in the Earth and if the remains of living things did fall into molten rock, the heat would destroy them and nothing would be left which could form a fossil. Fossils are occasionally found in metamorphic rock but because these rocks are formed by heat and pressure then the remains of the living things are often changed so much that it is hard to recognise them.

For you to try (page 126)

1 Investigation: Making a model solar system

- The main challenge in this investigation is to represent the solar system with a model that is to scale, especially since a pin head and a grain of rice are so small and difficult to see. Teachers and students should not worry about this but just do the best they can with whatever materials they have available.
- The distance between the planets is even more difficult to achieve on a piece of paper, but can be shown well in the next investigation.

2 Investigation: How far apart are the planets?

- The purpose of this investigation is for students to get some understanding of the relative distances between the planets.
- Mercury is the smallest planet and Jupiter is the largest.
- Mercury is the closest planet to the Sun and Neptune is the furthest.

For you to try (page 129)

1 Investigation: Night and day

This investigation will work best in a darkened room or on a day that is cloudy or when it is less bright. The torch should be powerful enough to illuminate the model globe. Drawing the continents on the model globe helps to make the investigation more realistic and to show the places where night and day is occurring. The person holding the model globe should make it rotate in an anti-clockwise direction since this is the direction in which the Earth spins.

2 Investigation: One year and the seasons

This investigation will work best in a darkened room or on a day that is cloudy or when it is less bright. The pressure lamp or electric lamp should give out light in all directions and be powerful enough to illuminate the model globe. Drawing the continents on the model globe helps to make the investigation more realistic and to show the places where different seasons are occurring.

I **One year** The Earth takes one year to make one orbit around the Sun and so the person holding the globe should walk in a circle around the lamp. To be more realistic the person should also rotate the globe on its axis in an anti-clockwise direction. The Earth rotates on its axis 365 times during one orbit of the Sun.

II **The seasons** In order to show the seasons the person holding the globe must tilt the Earth's axis to the plane of its orbit by about 23 degrees. This means that at any given time during summer or winter, one part of the planet is more directly exposed to the rays of the Sun. This exposure alternates as the Earth revolves in its orbit. At any time of the year the northern and southern hemispheres always experience opposite seasons.

The seasons are not caused by the variation in the Earth's distance to the Sun due to its elliptical orbit. This effect is small on Earth and other factors are more important. Scientists have found that the Earth is generally a few degrees warmer when it is farther from the Sun.

Some students may have difficulty understanding these ideas and teachers will also need to refer students to the diagrams in the student book and also draw them on the board.

Supplementary activities

g The rotation of the Earth on its axis causes day and night which has an important affect on people and other living things. Plants need sunlight so they can make food by the process of photosynthesis.

All animals depend on plants as the producers in a food chain. Day and night also affects the behaviour of many animals. For example, many animals are nocturnal and rest in the day time when it is hot but come out at night to feed when it is cooler. Day and night also affects the behaviour of human beings. Many human activities take place only in the day time and some activities make use of the dark, but, because humans have also learned to use artificial sources of light, activities that need light can also take place at night.

h The orbit of the Earth around the Sun causes the seasons, which have an important effect on people and other living things. People living in tropical countries, especially those nearest the equator, often experience a wet season and a dry season at a particular time each year and this is related to the position of the Earth during its orbit around the Sun. People living further from the equator in countries with a temperate climate will experience four seasons: spring, summer, autumn and winter. Each season will have different weather, especially temperature, and different lengths of day and night. People living in the northern hemisphere will experience the opposite season from people living in the southern hemisphere.

The season, and weather that comes with each, affects the crops that people can grow and the activities that they can do outside. Plants and animals are also affected by the seasons. For example, plants often grow best when the weather is warm and there is water available, but their growth may slow down and they may lose their leaves in the autumn. Some animals migrate with the seasons each year, moving north or south depending on the temperature. When it is very cold some animals hibernate during the winter.

For you to try (page 132)

1 Investigation: The phases of the Moon

- This investigation will work best in a darkened room or on a day that is cloudy or when it is less bright. The pressure lamp or electric lamp should give out light in all directions and be powerful enough to illuminate the model globe.
- The person playing the part of the Earth will most easily be able to see and understand the phases of the Moon and so students should take it in turns to play the part of the Moon.
- The new moon is when the Moon is all dark. None of the Moon that we can see is lit up during the new moon.
- The full moon is when the Moon is all lit up. All of the Moon that we can see is lit up by the Sun during the full moon.
- When it is a full moon the Sun and Moon are arranged in approximately a straight line on opposite sides of the Earth so the order is Sun, Moon, Earth.
- When it is a new moon the Sun and Moon are arranged in approximately a straight line on the same side of the Earth so the order is Sun, Earth, Moon.

For you to try (page 134)

1

- The total eclipses of the Sun in 1983 and 1984 were a major event for people living in parts of Central Province and Milne Bay. In 1983 the eclipse occurred on a Saturday afternoon so most people had time to observe what happened. In some parts of Port Moresby groups of friends gathered together and had eclipse parties to celebrate this special occasion. The weather was fine and people were able to notice the very significant difference during the time of totality, when the Sun was completely hidden. Roosters started crowing, birds came to roost in mango trees and dogs howled. One little girl who was being held in her father's arms and still learning to talk looked at the black disc hiding the Sun and said 'moon'. The eclipse lasted several minutes and when it was over people cheered.

- In Alotau in Milne Bay it was raining heavily and the sky was full of grey clouds. Unfortunately, people could not see the Sun and it was already very dull so although people could notice the effect of the eclipse, it could not be seen directly. However, people still noticed that plants and animals responded to the eclipse. For example, leaves of the rain tree that normally close their leaves when the sun sets at about 6 pm, closed their leaves even though it was the middle of the afternoon. Students on their way back to school from town were overheard saying that they thought that they were late because it was already getting dark.

2 The Moon takes about 28 days to rotate once on its own axis and also to complete one orbit of the Earth. This means that the same side of the Moon is always facing the Earth.

4 The phases of the Moon affect people and other living things on the Earth in a number of ways. The tides have a daily effect on people living near the sea and can affect the times that people go fishing, or the depth of water can affect the ability of a canoe or boat to be used in a lagoon or pass through a passage. The amount of moonlight can affect the activities of people who want to do things outside at night. The lunar calendar is also used to set the time of events such as Easter, Chinese New Year and Ramadan.

The behaviour of some animals that live in the sea can also be affected by the phases of the Moon. For example, coral usually spawn only once each year four to five days after the full moon in October or November. Eggs and sperm are released into the water and mix together. The palolo worm which is well known in Samoa and other Pacific islands also spawns once a year at this time. Eggs and sperm are again released into the water where fertilisation takes place. Palolo worms are considered as a special food and Samoans collect the worms at this time and eat them.

Projects (page 134)

1 Make a fossil collection

Making a fossil collection is easier if you live in an area where there are fossils, such as the limestone areas of the highlands. If you cannot find fossils locally you may be able to obtain some from people you know who are living in an area where there are fossils.

2 Make a sundial

A sundial is a device that measures time by the position of the Sun. The most commonly seen designs, such as garden sundials, cast a shadow on a flat surface marked with the hours of the day. As the position of the Sun changes, the time indicated by the shadow changes. However, sundials can be designed for any surface where a fixed object casts a predictable shadow.

Summary questions

1 C

2 C

3

Statement	T or F?
Fossils are the remains or evidence of living things that have been preserved.	T
Fossils are only found in rock.	F
Fossils can be formed in several ways.	T
Fossils will form only under special conditions.	T
Fossils can be found in igneous rock.	F
Fossils are very common because most of the animals that lived in the past have formed fossils.	F
Sedimentary rocks usually must be lifted up and then weathered before fossils can be found.	T

4 A

5

Word	Meaning or explanation	Answer
A Length of day	**I** Occurs because the Earth is tilted towards the Sun	C
B Night	**II** The Earth spinning once every 24 hours	A
C Season	**III** Time taken for the Earth to orbit the Sun once	D
D Year	**IV** Occurs on the part of the Earth facing away from the Sun	B

6

Term	Cause or explanation	Answer
A Low tide	**I** An extra large tide that occurs twice a month when the Sun, Moon and Earth are in line	D
B High tide	**II** A small tide that occurs twice a month when the Sun, Moon and Earth are at right angles to one another	C
C Neap tide	**III** A decrease in sea level that occurs twice a day on opposite sides of the Earth	A
D Spring tide	**IV** An increase in sea level that occurs twice a day on the side of the Earth closest to the Moon and on the opposite side of the Earth	B

7 A

8 B

9 **Rock** can be formed in different ways. For example, rock can be formed from volcanoes and from the **sediments** that are carried in water and settle on the bottom of the sea, lakes and swamps. The materials that make up rock can move in a **cycle.** Rock can be slowly **weathered** or worn away by water and wind and the small particles can be carried or **eroded** by water and settle down as sediments. Over thousands of years the sediment can form **layers** of sedimentary rock.

When plants and animals die they can become buried with the sediments and form **fossils.** Fossils are the preserved **remains** or traces of plants and animals that lived millions of years ago. Fossils can be used to work out how long ago a rock was **formed** and what plants and animals were living at that time.

Our solar system consists of eight **planets**, together with their moons, dwarf planets, asteroids, meteors and comets. We can observe changes in the **position** of the planets, the Moon and the Sun and these changes affect our way of life. The **tilt** of the Earth towards the Sun and the movement of the Earth around the **Sun** affect the length of day and night and the change of the **seasons**. The position of the Earth, Moon and Sun causes **tides**.

Appendices

Sample unit of work

This unit of work is just one way of integrating a number of learning outcomes from different strands and sub-strands of science in Grade 7. There are many ways that teachers can integrate learning outcomes, including from other subjects, to make a unit of work. Teachers need to develop units of work that meet the needs of the students and the community, and also suit their own teaching style. Just as we weave bilums from different kinds of material into different shapes and sizes to be used for different purposes, so different units of work can be planned and implemented, each with their own individual characteristics.

Sample unit
Title: Using energy to do work

Grade: 7
Timeframe: Eight weeks
Strand: Science in the home
Sub-strands:
- investigate how energy changes from one form to another (7.3.3)
- investigate how we use force in everyday life (7.3.4)
- identify and make recommendations on how simple machines can make life easier through community field study (7.3.5)

Purpose of the unit of work: to develop an understanding of the concept of energy and the way that energy can be used to do work in the community and make life easier.
Suggested links with other subjects or strands within science:
Personal Development: Strand: Our Culture, Lifestyle and Values
Social Science: Strand: Culture

Process skills	Student activities	Assessment	Number of lessons and estimated time
Investigating	• Observe and investigate the different ways people use energy • Identify and investigate forces that speed things up • Identify and investigate forces that slow things down • Design experiments to test forces e.g. to find out how a force can be used to slow the motion of an object • Investigate balanced and unbalanced forces using a rope with two groups of students • Investigate places nearby to find out how forces are applied e.g. workshops, wharves, road works, gardens • Research different types of forces and their effect on the community, both positive and negative • Conduct a survey to identify all the simple machines that people are using, the effect they have on the community and any new machines they would like to have	**Assessment task** List and classify different forms of energy. List different forces that act around us and their common characteristics. Write up a Scientific Report of an experiment or investigation to test forces. **Assessment criteria** The student correctly lists and classifies different sources of energy. The student correctly classifies different types of forces. Student satisfactorily designs and writes up an experiment using the headings Aim, Apparatus, Method, Results, and Conclusion.	10 × 40-minute lessons for activities 3 × 30-minute lessons for assessment
Comprehending	• Identify different forms of energy including heat and sound • Describe the different ways that simple machines make life easier • Describe the effects and characteristics of different forms of energy • Describe the energy changes that take place when using simple machines • List and describe different forces that act around us • Discuss different types of forces • Analyse findings from a survey on the use of simple machines and the need for new machines	**Assessment task** List and classify examples of energy changes that take place when using simple machines. Gather, summarise and interpret information from a survey on the use of simple machines and the need for new machines. **Assessment criteria** The student correctly identifies and describes the energy changes that take place when using simple machines. The student satisfactorily gathers, summarises and interprets survey information.	10 × 40-minute lessons for activities 3 × 30-minute lessons for assessment

Process skills	Student activities	Assessment	Number of lessons and estimated time
Communicating	• Prepare a written report on the advantages and disadvantages of friction. • Draw a poster to show the different ways people use energy such as heat, light and sound. • Make recommendations based on an analysis of the findings from the survey.	**Assessment task** Produce a labelled diagram or poster to show ways that people use energy. Analyse survey findings and make suitable recommendations. **Assessment criteria** Student chooses a relevant example, produces a clear diagram or poster, with appropriate heading and labels that communicates a message effectively. Student satisfactorily analyses findings from the survey and makes recommendations that are clearly related to the findings.	10 × 40-minute lessons for activities 3 × 30-minute lessons for assessment

Resources: *National Curriculum Statement, Science Upper Primary Syllabus 2003. Science Upper Primary Teachers Guide 2003, Grade 7 Student Book.*

Total estimated time for the unit of work: 30 × 40-minute teaching periods; 9 × 30-minute periods for assessment. (Total: 1470 minutes, that is, approximately the equivalent of eight weeks of work for science.)

Planning templates

Following are some sample templates that can be used for both long- and short-term planning.

Sample 1: Yearly plan

Units of work	Term 1	Term 2	Term 3	Term 4
Working scientifically	The scientific method	The scientific method	The scientific method	The scientific method
Living things	Basic structure of living things and how they function	Basic structure of living things and how they function	Relationships in a community and food webs	Relationships in a community and food webs
Science in the home	Structure and behaviour of matter	Properties of materials	Energy changes and forces	Simple machines in the home
Earth and beyond	Formation, composition and cycling of rocks	Sedimentary rocks and fossils	Interactions between the Earth, Moon and Sun	Interactions between the Earth, Moon and Sun

Sample 2: Term plan

Week	Student tasks	Required resources	Assessment procedures
1–3			
4–6			
7–10			

Sample 3: Lesson plan

Teaching group Individual Whole class Team group ✓	**Required materials**
Learning strategies Collaborating Interpreting Predicting ✓ Investigating Recording ✓ Justifying Changing Communicating	**Specific content—lesson plan**
Learning outcomes	**Assessment tasks**
Related outcomes from other subjects	**Integrated activities**

Assessment templates

Defining terms

Assessment refers to the collection and analysis of data about student behaviour and progress. Assessment data can also be used to make program decisions.

Evaluation refers to the process of using assessment information to make judgments about the effectiveness of teaching programs and to improve teaching practice so as to improve student learning.

Reporting refers to the procedures where assessment information is communicated to others (usually parents, students and other teachers) to inform and assist student learning.

Record-keeping is the documentation we keep when we assess and evaluate. Assessment information needs to be recorded in ways which enable the teacher to construct a profile of learning for each student.

An **Outcome** can be defined as a behaviour that students will demonstrate after learning experiences. Outcomes generally relate to knowledge and skills. Outcomes are usually broad and relate to long-term learning. Outcomes are demonstrable, sequential and observable.

Templates

The following templates are designed to give teachers suggestions on recording assessment information. They are not meant to be prescriptive, but to assist teachers in designing their own assessment records.

Sample 1: Skills assessment template

Science—skills checklist

Name: ______________________ **Date:** ______________

Topic	Skills	Achieved ✓			Comments
		Most of the time	Some of the time	Rarely	
Working scientifically	**Investigating** • Collect information • Explore phenomena • Seek reasons for happenings • Make a hypothesis • Look for patterns and meanings • Measure accurately • Access resources • Design experiments • Think carefully about problems • Make plans • Handle materials and equipment • Carry out investigations • Represent information • Use references • Cooperate with others				

Working scientifically	• Clarify and challenge values • Express a point of view • Listen actively • Formulate questions • Perform an experiment • Work safely **Comprehending** • Make decisions • Solve problems • Make predictions • Take actions • Classify using characteristics • Make oral and written reports • Think logically • Analyse and interpret information • Make suggestions • Use ideas, theories and principles • Construct meanings • Formulate and elaborate ideas • Make generalisations • Look for alternatives • Make comparisons • Make links • Apply ideas and concepts • Make judgments • Reflect • Draw conclusions • Examine and evaluate **Communicating** • Interpret information • Observe accurately • Create something new • Compare qualities of different things • Make models • Clarify ideas and concepts • Discuss with others • Listen and question • Respond and debate • Use scientific terminology • Negotiate with others • Support ideas • Argue a position • Construct models • Create presentations • Create tables and graphs • Summarise and report • Write and use scientific reports				
Living things	(Insert your own list of skills here)				
Science in the home	(Insert your own list of skills here)				
Earth and beyond	(Insert your own list of skills here)				

Sample 2: Cognitive skills template

Learning skills assessment checklist

For assessing learning skills, group communication skills and attitudes

Name: ______________________________ **Date:** ______________

Skills	Skills observed ✓	Comments
Learning skills • can form and ask questions • can follow instructions • can find information • can find required information • can express ideas clearly and correctly • can critically reflect on own work • can organise self efficiently • understands how to improve own work • manages use of time well		
Group skills • follows group rules • works cooperatively within a team • contributes to discussions without dominating • listens while other people speak • accommodates different points of view		
Attitudes • respects other students' point of view • participates freely in activities • works in a constructive and positive way • values the beliefs held by other students		

Sample 3: Student self-assessment template

Student self-assessment checklist

Name: ______________________________ **Date:** ____________________

Skills	Can do ✓
My learning skills • I can ask questions • I can follow instructions • I can find the information that I need • I can express myself clearly and correctly • I can think about what was right and wrong about my work • I can work neatly • I am well organised • I understand how to improve my work • I use my time well	
My group skills • I can work well with others in a group • I can listen when others are talking • I can discuss something without getting angry	
My attitudes • I can listen and respect what others have to say • I can take responsibility for my own work • I can share in a group activity • I can learn from my mistakes	
My comments	

Sample 4: Group assessment template

Group assessment

Date: ______________________

Name of group: ______________________

Names of group members:

____

____

Activity:

____

____

____

What things did your group do really well?

____

____

____

What things does your group need to improve?

____

____

____

What are you going to do to change the way your group works?

____

____

____

Sample 5: Term self-assessment template

My term report

Name: ____

I rate my working habits this term as:

I am a quiet worker	/10
I am a neat worker	/10
I finish my work on time	/10
I am able to work by myself	/10
I work well in groups	/10

What I did well this term

____

____

____

What I plan to improve on next term

____

____

____

What I would like to see changed next term

____

____

____

What I really liked doing this term

____

____

____

What I didn't like doing this term

____

____

____

Glossary

adaptation	the way a living thing has changed to make it more suitable for its way of life
adolescents	young people, usually teenagers, who have reached puberty but are not yet adults
algae	simple green plants that usually live in water or damp places e.g. seaweed
alloy	a metal made by mixing two or more different metals
amber	fossilised gum from a type of pine tree
amphibian	an animal that is able to live on land and in water by breathing through the skin and lungs e.g. frog
amylase	an enzyme that begins the chemical breakdown of starch during the process of digestion
andesite	a kind of igneous rock
archaeologist	a person who studies the past and the way that people lived by looking at the things left behind like pottery, tools etc.
asteroids	lumps of rock that are found in a belt between Mars and Jupiter
astronomy	the study of the planets, Sun, Moon, stars and the universe
atmosphere	the layer of gases that surrounds the Earth
atmospheric pressure	the weight of air pushing down on the Earth
atoms	the tiny particles from which all matter is made
axis	an imaginary line through the centre of the Earth
axle	a rod that is connected to the centre of a wheel and that allows the wheel to turn
basalt	a kind of igneous rock
bearings	machine parts that make surfaces roll over each other rather than sliding over each other
Big Bang	the idea or theory that the universe started with a big explosion
biodegradable	materials that can rot or be broken down by decay
biology	the study of living things like plants and animals
biomass	the total mass of each group of organisms in a food chain
boiling	the change of state that occurs when water changes into steam; the boiling point of water is 100°C
bony fish	fish that have a bony skeleton and scales all over the body
brass	an alloy made from copper and zinc
brittle	hard but breaks easily
bronze	an alloy made from copper and tin
camouflage	colours and patterns that make something difficult to see
canine	a pointed tooth that is used for gripping
carbohydrate	a food that contains starch, sugar or cellulose
carnivore	an animal that eats other animals e.g. spider
cartilaginous fish	fish that have a skeleton made of cartilage or gristle e.g. shark
casting	pouring liquid metal or plastic into a mould to make an object with a particular shape
cause	the reasons why something happens

cell membrane	the outer part of a cell that contains the cytoplasm
cells	the very small building blocks from which plants and animals are made
cellulose	the strong material that is found in plant cell walls
ceramics	pottery that is made from clay that has been heated to a high temperature
chemical change	a change that occurs to matter in which new substances are formed and energy is taken in or given out; also called a chemical reaction
chemistry	the study of substances like chemicals and medicines and the way that they behave
chlorophyll	the green substance found in plants that is used to make food
classification	putting things into groups according to their similarities and differences
clear felling	cutting down all the trees in the forest
coal	a hard, black substance that is formed underground from plants and animals that lived thousands of years ago; a type of fossil fuel
comet	a piece of rock and ice that orbits the Sun
community	all the living things in one habitat
compound	a substance that is made by joining one or two elements together
conclusion	something that you decide is true because you now know that other things are true
condensation	the change of state from gas to liquid
conductor	something that lets heat or electricity pass through easily
conifer	a plant that has exposed seeds in cones e.g. klinki pine
consumer	an animal that eats plants or other animals
control	the part of an experiment in which no changes are made so that the result can be compared with the test; *see also* test
crater	the round, hollow shape of the rim of a volcano or the shape left by a meteorite when it hits the ground
creation story	a way of explaining how something was made
crust	the outer layer of the Earth
decomposer	microbes such as bacteria and fungi that feed on the remains of dead plants and animals by making them rot or decompose
desalination	removing salt from water by distillation
development	the way in which living things grow and become bigger
digestion	the breakdown of large particles of food into small, simple particles
digestive system	a tube which starts at the mouth and ends at the anus that food passes through
dipstick	a special metal rod that is used to measure the level of oil in an engine
distillation	the process in which a liquid evaporates to a gas and then condenses back to a liquid; distillation can be used to separate substances; *see also* desalination
diverse	a natural environment that contains many different types of living things
ductile	can be pulled or stretched into wire
ear drum	a thin piece of skin inside the ear that can detect vibrations
eclipse	a shadow that hides part of the Sun or Moon
ecology	the study of the relationships and interactions between living things and their surroundings
ecosystem	a community and its environment
effect	something that happens as a result of something else

elastic	something which can stretch when a force is used and then return to its original shape and size
element	the simplest kind of matter that can exist on its own e.g. copper, gold, oxygen
elimination	passing faeces or undigested food out of the anus
energy	energy is the ability to do work; there are different types of energy
enzyme	a substance produced by a living organism that helps a chemical reaction to occur more easily
erosion	small pieces of weathered rock and soil that are carried away by water and wind
evaporation	the change of state from liquid to gas; a method used to separate a soluble solid from a solution
faeces	undigested food that passes out of the anus
fair	sensible, reasonable, logical
falling star	*see* shooting star
fern	a green plant that has no flowers but reproduces by producing spores on the underside of the fronds
fertiliser	a chemical that is added to the soil to make plants grow better
food chain	a feeding relationship in which one living thing feeds on another and that always begins with a plant
food web	a feeding relationship which is made up of a number of food chains; *see also* food chain
force	a push or a pull that usually makes something move or change direction
fossil	the remains of plants or animals that lived thousands of years ago
fossil fuel	coal, oil and natural gas that come from plants and animals that lived thousands of years ago
freezing	the change of state from liquid to solid; the freezing point of water is 0°C; *see also* solidification
friction	a force that slows things down or stops them moving; friction also allows things to grip so that they can move
fuel	a substance that can be burned to give energy
fungi	plants that have no chlorophyll but live on the dead remains of other plants and animals
galaxy	a large group of millions of stars
gas	matter that has no fixed volume and no fixed shape
gears	wheels with teeth around their edges that fit into the teeth of another wheel or into the holes of a chain
geology	the study of rocks and the Earth
geothermal	heat from the rocks in the Earth; electricity can be made from geothermal energy
gills	the organs that fish use to obtain oxygen from water
glacier	a slow moving river of ice
gnomon	the stick that casts a shadow on a sundial
granite	a kind of igneous rock
gravity	the force that pulls objects down
gullet	a tube that has muscles that move food from the mouth to the stomach

habitat	the place where an animal or plant lives in the environment
health	the study of the reasons why we get sick and how we can get better
herbivore	an animal that eats plants e.g. butterfly
humus	decaying plants and animals
hypothesis	a possible explanation that has not been proved
igneous rock	rock formed from magma that has cooled and solidified at the Earth's surface (volcanic rock) or deep within the Earth's surface (plutonic rock)
imprint	the shape left behind by a plant or animal
incisor	sharp-edged, chisel-like tooth at the front of the mouth used for biting off pieces of food
incline	a slope
index fossil	a fossil that can help to work out the age of the rock in which it is found
inertia	the way in which heavy objects do not move easily or are difficult to stop when they are moving
inference	a type of conclusion and possible explanation
insoluble	something that does not dissolve
insulator	something that stops heat or electricity passing through
intestine	part of the digestive system; *see also* small intestine *and* large intestine
invertebrate	an animal that does not have a backbone
kilojoule	a unit of energy, equal to 1000 joules; the symbol for kilojoule is kJ
kinetic energy	moving energy
lane	the lines on a running track that show a runner where to run
large intestine	part of the digestive system where water is absorbed into the bloodstream
lever	a simple machine that can be used to make work easier; a lever is usually a strong, rigid bar or rod
liquid	matter that has a fixed volume but no fixed shape
liverwort	a simple green land plant that lives in cool, damp places
logging	cutting down trees as part of the timber industry
lubricant	a solid or liquid that reduces friction e.g. oil or grease
lubrication	adding oil or grease so that the surfaces of moving parts slide over each other more easily
lunar eclipse	an eclipse of the Moon that occurs when the shadow of the Earth moves across the Moon
lunar month	the time taken for the Moon to go through one cycle of light and dark shapes and which lasts 28 days
machine	something that helps to make work easier
magma	molten rock inside the Earth
magnet	a piece of iron or steel that attracts iron or steel towards it
malleable	can be hammered into shape
mammal	an animal that has fur or hair on the body and two pairs of limbs; *see also* marsupial, monotreme *and* placental
marsupial	a mammal in which the young develop in a pouch e.g. wallaby, bandicoot, possum
mass	the quantity of substance or amount of material in something

matter	any material or substance that has mass and takes up space
meteor	pieces of matter that move around the solar system
meteorite	a meteor that reaches the surface of the Earth
meteorology	the study of the weather
melting	the change of state from solid to liquid
metal	solids that are usually hard and can be flattened into sheets and stretched into wires
metamorphic rock	rock that has been changed because of high temperature and pressure; it is harder and looks different
Milky Way	the galaxy with a spiral shape in which we live
mineralisation	the process in which the minerals in a fossil are replaced with minerals from water and sediment so that a copy is made which looks like rock
mixture	something that contains at least two separate substances
molar	large tooth at the back of the mouth that is used for crushing; *see also* premolar
molten	rock or metal that has been heated to a very high temperature and has become a thick sticky liquid
monotreme	a mammal that lays eggs e.g. echidna, platypus
moss	a simple green land plant that lives in cool, damp places
mould	a shape or hole which is left by the body of an animal in mud, clay or ash; when the hole is filled it becomes a cast which has the same shape as the original animal
moult	to lose the outer skin which is replaced by the new skin underneath e.g. lizards and insects
neap tide	the lowest tide which occurs during the first quarter and last quarter of the Moon
non-renewable	something that cannot easily be replaced
observation	something that you notice using any of your senses
obsidian	a hard, shiny black igneous rock that can be used to make sharp tools
omnivore	an animal that eats both plants and animals e.g. pig, human being
organ	a part of the body that is made up of two or more different kinds of tissue that work together to carry out a particular job e.g. the heart
organism	an animal or a plant; any living thing
particles	the tiny parts or atoms from which all matter is made
pesticide	a chemical that is used to kill insects and other pests
phases of the Moon	different shapes of the Moon seen from the Earth
photosynthesis	the process in which plants make their own food using sunlight
physical change	a change that occurs to matter in which no new substances are formed
physics	the study of forces and movement, energy and matter, tools and machines
placental	a mammal in which the young develop inside the mother's womb before being born alive e.g. dog, pig, human, whale
plane	a surface
planet	a body that moves in orbit around the Sun; there are eight planets in our solar system
plankton	tiny plants that live in water and are the producers in many food chains
population	a group of animals or plants of the same kind

potential energy	stored energy
predator	an animal that catches and eats other animals
premolar	large tooth at the back of the mouth that is used for crushing; *see also* molar
prey	the animals that predators eat
producer	a plant
products	things that are made from naturally occurring materials; the new substances that are formed in a chemical reaction
properties	the way in which a substance or object behaves
protease	an enzyme that breaks down complex protein to simple protein
pulley	a simple machine that consists of a rope, chain or belt stretched over the rim of a wheel
pumice	a very light igneous rock that can float on water
pure	one substance that exists by itself
radiant energy	energy that can travel through space and air in the form of electro-magnetic rays
rain shadow	an area that receives less rain because of the way in which the wind is pushed up and over mountains which makes the rain fall in a different place
raw materials	naturally occurring materials that are used to make products
reactants	the original substances that are used up in a chemical reaction
reliable	information that is honest and true so that we can believe it
reptiles	cold-blooded animals that have a dry, scaly skin and lungs that live mainly on the land e.g. snakes, crocodiles, turtles
resource	something that can be used to meet the needs of people
respiration	the process in which plants and animals get energy from food
rock cycle	the processes of rock formation, uplift, weathering and erosion that occur in the Earth's crust
root	the part of a flowering plant that is below the ground
rotation	the spinning of the Earth on its axis
ruminant	a herbivore that can chew its food several times and also has bacteria in its stomach that can help to split open plant cells during digestion
satellite	something that orbits or travels around the Sun
saturated solution	a solution in which no more solute will dissolve in the solvent
scavenger	an animal that feeds on dead organisms
science	a way of finding out and understanding the world around us
scientific method	a way of working and solving problems
scientific processes	the steps that we follow to find out things
scientists	people who work in science
season	a period of time that has characteristic weather and day length
sediment	small particles of solid that settle at the bottom of a liquid
sedimentary rock	rock that is formed from sediments that have been compressed
selective logging	cutting down only certain types and sizes of trees
shoot	the part of a flowering plant that is above the ground
shooting star	a meteor that burns up as it enters the Earth's atmosphere leaving a fiery tail

skeleton	the part of an animal that provides support; some animals have an internal skeleton made of bones, and some have an external skeleton, such as insects
small intestine	part of the digestive system where a little mechanical breakdown of food takes place and a lot of chemical digestion
solar	from the Sun
solar eclipse	an eclipse of the Sun that occurs when the Moon comes between the Sun and the Earth so that parts of the Earth are in the Moon's shadow
solar still	a way of obtaining fresh water from salty water by using distillation and energy from the Sun
solar system	the Sun and the family of eight planets, moons and asteroids
solder	an alloy made from lead and tin
solid	matter that has a fixed volume and a fixed shape
solidification	the change of state from liquid to solid; *see also* freezing
soluble	able to dissolve
solute	a substance that dissolves in a liquid
solution	a mixture in which one substance is dissolved in another
solvent	a liquid that can dissolve things e.g. water
spring tide	the highest tide which usually occurs at full moon and new moon
staggered start	different positions on the curved part of a running track at the beginning of a race so that all runners cover the same distance
stainless steel	an alloy made from iron, chromium, manganese and nickel
state	the condition of matter—whether it is a solid, liquid or gas
stem	part of the shoot of a flowering plant that supports the leaves, buds, flowers and fruits
stomach	the organ where mechanical digestion takes places using muscles that churn food around to break it into smaller pieces
streamlined	a smooth shape that reduces friction when something moves through water or air
strong	something that resists the effects of forces
substance	any material from which things are made
sundial	a simple clock that uses the Sun to tell the time of day
suspension	a mixture of small particles of insoluble solid and a liquid; *see also* sediment
system	a group of organs and tissues that work together to carry out a particular job e.g. circulatory system
territory	an area in which an animal lives and that it will guard or defend
test	the part of an experiment in which changes are made so that the result can be compared with the control; *see also* control
thinning	removing plants that look weak so that the remaining plants get more nutrients and grow better
tide	a change in sea level that is caused by the gravitational pull of the Moon on the Earth
tissue	a group of cells that are similar to each other e.g. skin tissue
traditional knowledge	the understanding of processes and materials that people have used to live successfully
transparent	lets light through or 'see-through'

turbulent	water or air that is constantly moving and changing direction
universe	the whole of space and all the stars and planets and everything in space
uplift	movements in the Earth which push up the rocks to form mountains
variation	differences in the equivalent structures of a group of living things, such as roots
vegan	a person who does not eat meat or fish, or any animal products like milk, butter or cheese
vegetarian	a person who does not eat meat or fish
vertebrate	an animal that has a backbone
vibration	moving quickly backwards and forwards
water cycle	the movement of water in the environment which includes precipitation, evaporation and condensation
weathering	the slow breaking down of rock into smaller pieces
webbed feet	having skin between the toes
wedge	something which is thick at one end and thin at the other e.g. the head of an axe
weight	the downward pull of the Earth's gravity on the mass of an object

Teacher notes

Teacher notes